NADDER

TALES OF A WILTSHIRE VALLEY

*There were hilles which garnished
their proud heights with stately
trees; humble valleis, whose base
estate seemed comforted with the
refreshing of silver rivers;
meadows, enameld with al sorts of
ey-pleasing floures; thickets,
which being lined with most
precious shade, were witnessed so
to by the chereful disposition of
many wel-tuned birds; each pasture
stored with sheep, feeding with
sober security. . .*

Philip Sidney *Arcadia*

Nadder

Tales of a Wiltshire Valley

REX SAWYER

EAST KNOYLE
THE HOBNOB PRESS

This is a revised edition of *Tales of a Wiltshire Valley: the Nadder,* first published in 1995 by Alan Sutton Publishing Ltd.

This edition published in the United Kingdom in 2006 by Hobnob Press, PO Box 1838, East Knoyle, Salisbury SP3 6FA

British Library Cataloguing in Publication Data
A catalogue record for this book is available from the British Library.

ISBN 10   0-946418-53-5
ISBN 13 (from January 2007) 978-0-946418-53-4

Typeset in 11/15 pt Scala, Futura and Colonna
Typesetting and origination by John Chandler
Printed in Great Britain by Salisbury Printing Company Ltd, Salisbury

The frontispiece illustration is a mid-19th century painting of the Cross at Chilmark by an unknown artist.

The front cover illustration is of Teffont Evias, the back cover illustration is of Place Farm, Tisbury (both photographs by John Chandler)

Contents

to Warminster

to Wylye

A303

GROVELY

A36

Berwick St Leonard

Fonthill Bishop

B3089

Teffont Magna

Baver- stock

Barford St Martin

Hindon

Chilmark

B3089

Dinton

A30

East Knoyle

Fonthill Gifford

Teffont Evias

Wilton

Salisbury

Tisbury

Fovant

Burcombe

A350

Sutton Mandeville

A30

Compton Chamberlayne

old road

Semley

Swallowcliffe

WARDOUR

Ansty

scale of ten kilometres

Donhead St Mary

Donhead St Andrew

A30

Shaftesbury

Introduction

WHEN JOHN LELAND, the Tudor topographer, referred to the Nadder as Fovington Water because 'it risith about Fovington [Fovant] village', he was sadly awry. Traditionally its source has been given as Nadder Head, several miles further west, among the ponds of Wincombe Park near Shaftesbury. If this is so, the initial stream soon receives reinforcements, for the whole area of the Donheads is alive with springs. Several arise in the chain of hamlets known as the Coombes. Another gushes forth to form Bob Williamson's cressbeds at Ludwell and is often referred to as the River Don. Many more can be seen from his nearby home, Mill House, where they weep freely from the hillside. Ferne Brook and the River Sem near Wardour also converge to ensure that by the time it reaches Tisbury, the Nadder is a river of respectable dimensions.

The Nadder derives its name from the Saxon *naedre* meaning a 'snake'. An aerial view confirms this as a very apt description as there is hardly a straight stretch between the Donheads and Wilton, where it joins the Wylye and then the Avon on its way to Christchurch and the open sea.

Beloved of anglers, walkers and naturalists alike, the Nadder Valley has clearly defined limits. To the south lie the chalk downlands which, with their key points of Win Green and White Sheet Hill, define the outer boundary of Cranborne Chase. To the north, a similar range of hills, shrouded by the woodland of Grovely and Great Ridge, separates the Nadder from the Wylye. Along each the trackways of earlier civilisations pass to the west.

Within these boundaries, the limestone villages of the Nadder lie either side of the river among scenery of gentle wooded hills and luxuriant pastures. Described by Ralph Whitlock as perhaps the loveliest of all the valleys of Salisbury Plain, it is not surprising that many buildings of elegance and historical significance can be found. Chief among these are the homes of the Arundells at Wardour and the Pembrokes at Wilton, the most powerful of its landowners since the Dissolution of the Monasteries.

The rich strata of Portland and Purbeck stone, especially at Chilmark and Tisbury, provided the main building material not just for the big houses but for the homes of merchants, farmers and the ordinary cottagers upon whom the whole valley economy depended. This book attempts to reveal something of their lives as well as those dwelling in marbled halls. In particular it will concentrate on the last one hundred to one hundred and fifty years – the period of greatest change in our history – when the customary existence of villagers was to be dramatically transformed.

Perhaps I should emphasise that I am not an expert on the Nadder Valley. To be so would require far more experience of geology, botany and other natural sciences than I can claim. This book has no pretensions of being the academic study that such specialists might compile. At times I have found myself straying across the vaguely defined line which separates history from folklore. It is the combination of the two which is so engrained in the fabric of each village and creates their separate mythologies. Nevertheless, I have kept

the Rubicon well in mind and had each chapter reviewed by someone from each village whose opinion I respect. To them must go my first thanks.

Not surprisingly, there are many institutions – the village band, the slate club, each jubilee and coronation celebration – that are held in common. To record them slavishly would make for tedious reading. I have tried to maintain some balance by a process of selection, referring to them when most appropriate to the text. Change brings its own problems and I have also tried to highlight those which Nadder Valley communities, as well as others, have had to face for the future.

Above all, this is a book about the people of the Nadder Valley. In a sense, they have written it themselves and I am deeply grateful to them. Many are acknowledged at the end of this book for the time and trouble they have taken. In particular I should like to acknowledge my appreciation to the late Rex Galpin who painstakingly copied over three hundred and eighty prints, kindly loaned, in order to produce the ones finally selected.

I wish to express my appreciation to Dr John Chandler who in a busy professional life found time to read the entire text, to John Pope who produced the Nadder Valley map, to Bruce Purvis and Judith Giles at Salisbury Local Studies Library for their helpful assistance with my queries, and to my wife, Sheila, for her constant encouragement and support.

Not surprisingly, since this book was first published a decade ago, there have been further changes in the Nadder

Valley.   Some have been extensions to the evolving village scene; others, due to the inevitable ebb and flow of human existence.   In the natural course of things, most of the people whose testimony so enlivened our picture of the valley during the early 20th century, have now died.   Their descriptions of rural life before the dramatic changes to the way we live now are therefore of more value and my gratitude to them the greater.

As for my personal agenda, may I leave you with the following thoughts with which the study has left me:

■ Why has the vitality been sapped from so many village institutions – the W.I., the Young Wives Club, girl guides, cubs and scouts, the cricket team and many others?

■ Are we going to regret the fact that many of our rural light industrial sites have been converted into residential use?

■ How will we establish a new social cohesion when all the indigenous families (whose children can no longer afford to live here) as well as pubs, shops, the Post Office and other social meeting places have disappeared?

Rex Sawyer
Tisbury

1

Donhead
the Head of the Downs

L YING WITHIN THE OUTER RIM of Cranborne Chase,
the two parishes of Donhead St Mary and Donhead
St Andrew combine to form the Donheads, a
beautiful area of contrasting high chalk downs, of which Win
Green is the crowning glory, and wooded coombs within
which lie houses of great antiquity. The twin parishes form
the extreme western end of the Nadder Valley and are linked
by the most bewildering network of narrow twisting lanes.

In the Middle Ages, the two formed one large estate
called Donhead – the Head of the Downs – although the
boundary had apparently been drawn between them as early
as the 11th century. Granted by King Alfred to the Abbesses
of Shaftesbury, it remained with them until the Dissolution

when Sir Thomas Arundell, living at nearby Wardour Castle, became Lord of the Manor, an association which has continued, remarkably, until the present day.

Donhead St Mary has previously been known as Upper or Over Donhead to distinguish it from its neighbour (which, ironically, embraces the higher ground). It contains the hamlets of Ludwell, Charlton and the mysterious chain of low-lying homesteads known as the Coombes. Here, memorial stones to members of the Pond family are grim reminders of the 1665 plague epidemic.

Travelling southwards from Semley Hill you will pass the prehistoric remnants of Castle Rings and descend the Sticklepath to Gutch Common. As you enter Donhead St Mary you will find The Shute, once the only regular source of water for human and animal alike. Now the source has been diverted, leaving a residue to seep sluggishly from beneath the wall.

The Sheepwash at Ludwell, early 20th century

Below The Shute, the lane approaches the imposing tower of St Mary's Church. Here, in a loop between Church Hill and Watery Lane, lies the heart of the old village, its shops and ancient work places restored and infilled by more recent dwellings.

Watery Lane, where Nadder tributaries intrude in wetter seasons, is aptly named. After a period of prolonged rain it comes alive with liquid activity. Water seeps from the banks into narrow channels on either side and rushes by with a melodious chatter. The lane, too, is awash with a succession of milky waves.

St Mary's Church was originally Norman and of modest proportions but like so many churches it has been enlarged with the increase in population. The two side chapels and the tower, for example, were added in the 14th century. The chancel has macabre figures at prayer engraved in a side pillar and the Jacobean altar, too, is richly carved with strange creatures writhing among foliage. A French Carthusian monk, one of five who took refuge in Coombe Abbey during the French Revolution, was 'banished from his country for religion' and is commemorated on a tablet in the south wall of the tower.

The outer hamlets of Charlton, Ludwell and the Coombes are served by a second church, St John's. It was built in 1839 to replace an earlier medieval chapel in Charlton village where, until 1638, the ancient custom was practised of each communicant bringing to the altar from his own home an offering of bread and wine for Communion.

Near Win Green there is a Quaker cemetery, perhaps the earliest physical evidence of Donhead's strong Nonconformist tradition. It is kept open by driving a wagon down the track once every decade. Quakers today must make their way to Shaftesbury to worship but evidence of other dissenters still abounds.

Donhead Hall is entered by a modest gateway at the bottom of Watery Lane. It is a handsome Grade II listed mansion of the early Georgian period, refreshingly little altered except for a Victorian glass-domed entrance at the side. Little is known of its chequered past. Reputedly built as a wedding present, it originally had a drive that curved up to the front entrance with a steep drop to the left. A carriage and four overturned, killing the lady of the house after which the drive was altered to a safer route at the side. It once belonged to

the illegitimate son of Sir Godfrey Kneller, the famous Dutch painter of the courts of William of Orange and George I. Having married the heiress of Donhead Hall, the son then took his father's name by Act of Parliament in 1731.

During the 20th century the house sank into decay, its fabric neglected and its splendid orangery lacking a roof. On all sides nature had encroached. A pack of twenty or so pedigree Pekinese, pets of a previous owner, laid waste to the interior. A more recent owner, Charles McVeigh, determined to return it to its original splendour, restoring the orangery and renovating the magnificent Georgian façade.

William Ingram, a Donhead man, was transported for life in 1836 for stealing a ewe, but by that time convict labour had virtually ceased in the colonies. With huge areas of land

opposite] Watery Lane Farm, Donhead St Mary, pre-1904. Home of the Burt family (Edwin and Sarah) whose daughter Meline married the market gardener Reuben Peckham

ripe for settlement, however, there was still a desperate shortage of labour for agriculture and trade. At the same time many were living close to poverty in England, especially as the increased mechanisation of the Industrial Revolution seriously reduced rural employment. Neither could the local authorities, with the reorganisation of the Poor Law in 1834, afford the money to support the families of the unemployed.

Through economic necessity, therefore, many poor families looked to the new colonies. At a meeting of Donhead ratepayers in 1836 it was decided to borrow £100 to send some villagers 'being willing to emigrate' to North America. One hundred and ninety-one accepted and two years later a still larger scheme sent others to New South Wales, a list of willing applicants being obtained from the Clerk of Tisbury Union where Donhead paupers were lodged.

The descendants of these early settlers still show a keen interest in their origins. One of them, Martin Smith, descended from two of the original Donhead families, wrote to the Vicar of Shaftesbury in 1985 asking for help in tracing his ancestors. Those enquiries led to the formation of the Australian Association of Donhead Descendants. Their monthly newsletters from 1985 to 1987 are full of interesting information concerning the village, past and present – a remarkable testimony to a people's desire to reach across the world and one hundred and fifty years to seek out their origins, and to the present inhabitants who responded so warmly.

The difficulties of travel through the steep winding lanes of the Donheads, badly affected by flood and frost in hard weather, ensured that they remained a self-contained community until well into the 20th century. In addition to the seven water-mills, one a fulling mill at Ludwell, there was a plethora of trades servicing the agricultural and domestic needs of the area. The absorbing Women's Institute Scrapbook of 1956 records an active wagon works at Birdbush, watercress beds, sawpits, numerous bakers' shops, a boot mender – even a rake and basket maker in Brookwater. A brewery existed at Donhead St Mary and at Ludwell a saddle maker flourished. The blacksmith and two wheelwright shops recorded would have been of fundamental importance to the local farmers and tradesmen who remained dependent on horse-drawn transport until well after the First World War. Women worked in the fields, became laundresses or domestic servants. A flourishing cottage industry of glove making existed with a collection and distribution point at Arundell Farm, once the Glove Inn, on the A30.

Fred Peckham was the third generation of a flourishing market gardening business centred on Church Hill. He has no illusions about how hard life could be:

> Father was born the wrong side of the blankets! It's no disgrace today but was considered so then. He was brought here as a baby and left on the doorstep of my grandfather William Arnold who was a widower. Father's name was Reuben Peckham (after his mother) and when he was

William Arnold, founder of a market gardening business at Church Hill, Donhead St Mary, in the latter half of the 19th century.

Reuben Peckham, 1897. He carried on the market garden business of his father, William Arnold, at Church Hill, Donhead St Mary. A devout Baptist, he brought up his six children very strictly, and thought about nothing but his religion and work.

fourteen his father started him going to Salisbury twice a week with a donkey and cart. When he had two donkeys he thought he was lord of the manor!

In 1888 he married my mother Meline, a member of the Burt family from Watery Lane Farm. When I was six months old we moved from Hope Cottage, at Jenkins Corner, to Church Hill. There were now six children and we were never allowed out into the road or to play any games. My earliest memories were of the chapel, mother and father being strict Wesleyan Methodists. Each Sabbath consisted of Sunday school 10.45 am, main service at 11 am, most likely preacher for lunch, Sunday school 2.45 pm and service again at 6 pm. During the First World War soldiers came to the evening service from Fovant and gathered round the harmonium afterwards for the singing of Sankey's 'Songs and Solos'.

We were never friends with father. In fact we were afraid of him until he was an old man and opened up more. He only thought of one thing and that was work. After school we had to get into older clothes and were allocated jobs, the girls house-cleaning, the boys cleaning the stables and the harness, greasing the carts, boiling the pigs' potatoes, cutting chaff and pulping roots.

Ernest, my elder brother, was a man when he was fourteen and going to Salisbury market regularly. Before market days father would stay up all night getting everything ready. By the time I was old enough to start father was no longer going but still stayed up to have the

Percy, Cissie and Annie
Goddard from Watery Farm,
Donhead St Mary

horses ready by the gate for us to leave at 2 am and would
bring the trace horse as far as Overway.

    We travelled through the Chalke Valley in those days
as it wasn't considered safe to go through the army camp at
Fovant. We got into Salisbury about 7 am and put the
horses in the stables belonging to the Catherine Wheel
which were in Penny Farthing Street. Then to Mrs Field's
Café in the Market Place. She served all the market people
from about 5 am. The wagon was always opposite Style and
Gerrishes [now Debenhams], always backwards to the kerb
to make it easier to unload. Before starting for home at
about five in the evening, we went into Exeter Street for a
loaf from the baker's and a piece of cheese. We made our
way slowly back and arrived home between 9 and 10 pm
having seen Wyatts, the bakers at Alvediston, just starting
the next day's round!

Sarah and Edwin Burt from
Watery Farm, Donhead St
Mary, early 20th century.

Em Dunston lived her life at Burltons, a small manor house with charming views across the Vale of Wardour. The Dunstons came from 'the old-fashioned gentry', their memorial stones decorating the walls of St Mary's Church. An interesting impressionistic stained-glass window dedicated to her parents can be seen in the southern side chapel. Em ran the local library with her sister Camilla and was an active leader of cultural life over several mid-century decades. More importantly for us, she recorded in dialect prose and poetry the life and characters of a Donhead now long gone. These individuals, products of the 'old' village life, indicate something of the colour and vitality that has been lost outside the pages of a Hardy novel. One of these was George Arnold.

Described in the 1891 Census as a coal haulier of Lower Wincombe, George kept a string of donkeys and little rough carts with which he hauled sacks of coal from Semley station three miles away up a very steep hill. If he put too heavy a load on the donkeys, which he often did, he used to harness his wife and daughters to the shaft and make them pull whilst he walked at the side! Eventually they could endure this behaviour no longer and, not surprisingly, left him to carry on alone. This he did for a long time until he fell ill and could no longer work.

The night he died, a great loneliness must have overtaken him for in the morning the neighbours, peeping through the uncurtained windows, saw the old man dead with his arms around one of his donkeys' necks. In his

Em Dunston holding a Samian bowl found in her garden at Burltons, Donhead St Mary. Em's family lived in the village for generations, their memorial stones decorating the walls of St Mary's Church. She recorded the life and characters of the 'old' Donhead village in Wiltshire dialect.

misery and fear of death, he must have fetched in the donkey to keep him company.

Hugh Maidment was recorded by Em as a wonderful old countryman. 'To see him in his prime mowing a field of grass was as good as watching a ballet dancer, the graceful swing from his hips and the wide swift movement of his scythe was a pleasure to behold.' It was said that in the hayfields he used to swallow small frogs whole 'to tarryfy the maidens'. In later age he injured himself somehow and walked with a hook stick around his neck to keep it rigid.

John Trowbridge, another old countryman, is described as one of the last wearers of the picturesque smock frock. He was often seen leaning on his stick, followed by his dog, the pockets of his frock stuffed with rosy apples for any children he might meet. He lived with his old brother-in-law, 'Baa-Lamb', who, dressed in a long seamed coat with two buttons behind, his head crowned with a tall, rough beaver hat and his thin legs encased in long drab gaiters, must have turned every head.

Charlton Church was at one time remarkable in having a blind organist and a deaf choir master, William Hobbs the schoolmaster. The organist was Jimmy Sharp remembered by Fred Peckham as the miller at West End. He damaged himself with a knife while cutting string on a sack as a young man, but continued to work the mill into old age.

Many are the tales stored up and recorded by Em in the WI Scrapbook. They tell of the ancient remedies for sickness, of village superstitions, witches and the smugglers from Poole craftily using the locals' fear of ghosts to peddle their contraband far inland. The lighting of bonfires on Win Green, morris dancing and the 'skimmity ride', torch-light processions on Gunpowder Night, all bear witness to a richness of village life sharply contrasted with the self-contained villa existence of the late 20th century:

> The wold school bell do idle hang
> Us hears no more his merry clang
> No more the zound o' pattrin' veet
> Comes runnin' up the village street.
> A girt red 'bus do whirl aroun'
> And takes they chill'ens off to Town.

I liked to zee they little maids
In pinners, wi' their hair in braids.
But now, no pinners 'ere be worn
And gold'n heads be permed or shorn.
Boys went a-nestin', nuttin' too,
And little maids picked vi'lets blue
Ah well! Times change, and so do we,
And yet I think as you'll agree
We've lost zumart in old world ways.

Em Dunston

~ ~ ~

Jimmy Sharp the blind miller from West End Mill, Donhead St Mary, early 20th century. He was also the organist in the church at Charlton. He damaged his eyes with a knife cutting string on a sack.

Donhead St Andrew lies on the opposite bank of the Nadder, another large straggling village similarly endowed with twisty lanes, far-flung hamlets and secretive houses of great charm. Its heart, however, lying in a hollow where the river, running beneath the road, fringes the church and school, could easily be missed. Vicar here from 1954 to 1979 was the scholar John Godfrey, whose church pamphlet encapsulates the village in the most succinct prose.

The village appears to have been quite rich in literary connections. John Godfrey reminds us that the 16th-century author Philip Sidney had a great fondness for the Nadder Valley. It may well have influenced his writing of *Arcadia,* a pastoral romance written at Wilton House between 1580 and 1581. The lines quoted at the beginning of this book are certainly an apt description of the Donheads.

The young poet Shelley had family connections with the Grove family at Ferne House and enjoyed a brief but passionate liaison with his cousin, Harriet Grove. William Lisle Bowles, another early 19th-century poet, lived in the village for a time and was visited by his friend, Samuel Taylor Coleridge.

Later still, the writer Thomas Hardy enjoyed a mild flirtation with Agnes Grove, also from Ferne House and a daughter of the pioneer archaeologist General Pitt Rivers from the nearby Rushmore Estate. He wrote his last sonnet, 'Concerning Agnes', when he heard of her death whilst he himself was in his eighties:

> I am stopped from hoping what I have hoped before –
> > Yes, many a time! –
> To dance with that fair woman yet once more
> > As in the prime
> Of August, when the wide-faced moon looked through
> The boughs at the faery lamps of the Larmer Avenue . . .

The position of St Andrew's Church, low down by the Nadder, gave rise to the terms Lower, or Nether, Donhead by which the settlement around the church was known in the 17th century. Thought to be of Saxon origin, the dominance of the abbesses of Shaftesbury is remembered today by one small piece of medieval glass depicting the arms of the abbey at the top of the east window. After the Dissolution the estates passed to the Arundells at Wardour Castle.

A paper in the church records the story of James Whitney, a well-respected rector of St Andrew's who was removed from office after the puritan Civil War by the Puritan Committee of Salisbury. He was replaced by Rector Legg, the son of a butcher, and lived on charity with his wife until regaining his living after the Restoration. When asked how he did. Mr Whitney would often reply, 'Very well, I thank God, only I am troubled by a very bad Legg!' Hardly surprising as his successor was reputed to be a turbulent, haughty and ill-natured fellow who treated his father, the butcher, so badly that 'he either hanged

Donhead

Shaftesbury Fire Brigade arriving four hours after being called to a fire at Whitesands Cross, Donhead St Andrew, in the 1920s. Cartoon drawn by Mr Wilmot, the Shaftesbury chimney sweep.

himself or as the neighbours say, was hanged by his son, on his order'.

A memorial tablet in the church is a fitting tribute to Captain John Cooke, who lived across the river in Donhead Lodge. After a distinguished career he was killed at an early stage of the Battle of Trafalgar, his ship *Bellerophon* later taking Bonaparte to his final captivity on St Helena.

To the west of the church lies Donhead House, previously the rectory. The last rector to live there was Horace Chapman who converted to Catholicism and enlarged the house to its present size in 1895. The lines of the original Queen Anne rectory can clearly be seen from the lawn. Chapman's daughter married a young cavalry officer who later became Lord Allenby of Palestine during the First World War. John Godfrey, in his village pamphlet, recalls an old Donhead chorister telling him how red carpeting was laid all the way from the rectory door, through the gate and across the lane to the church.

Later, Donhead House became the home of Sir Anthony Eden, the post-Churchillian prime minister, for a short time after his retirement from political life. He was searching for his own estate and eventually found it at Alvediston (or 'ell-of-a-distance' as the natives call it!) in the adjoining Ebble Valley. Donhead House was then owned by Rank Hovis McDougall as a training college and experimental farm before the estate was broken up and the house returned to private residence.

Completing this cluster of older buildings around the church, now supplemented by a plethora of modern houses, is the school built in 1880. By 1938, however, numbers had declined to fifty-eight and further decreases in village population led to its closure in 1970. Donhead St Andrew is fortunate, however. The purchase of the school building by the Henrietta Barnett School in London as a study centre has ensured its survival. It is a fine partnership. Not only does it supply a useful learning experience for the girls from London but the village enjoys the use of the premises as a part-time social centre.

The southern boundary of Donhead St Andrew lies along the chalk downland where you can walk the Ox Drove, an ancient trackway to the top of the 700 ft Win Green. Below this to the west of Berwick St John lies the plantation of Ferne. Until recently, a conglomeration of stables and outhouses was all that was left to remind us of a once great estate and a quite extraordinary 20th-century venture.

From 1563, Ferne remained in the hands of the Grove family, large landowners in the area with a fine town house at Shaftesbury. The family is still commemorated in the area by the Grove Arms, the old coaching inn at Ludwell. During the disturbed period of the Commonwealth and after, Thomas Grove, a strong parliamentarian, allowed Ferne to be used as a sanctuary for dissenters. One of these was Peter Ince, the displaced rector from Donhead St Mary.

Throughout the 18th century the Grove family continued to grow in wealth and political influence. In Victorian times this culminated in a baronetcy for Thomas Grove, like

Ferne House, with staff, the Revd. Mitchell and war refugee children. Vi Head's husband, Fred, is in the long coat. He worked as a gardener and odd job man. Her sister, Frances Dykes, holding the two dogs, was in service at Ferne for forty years.

so many of his predecessors, MP for the area. His son Walter's marriage to the daughter of General Pitt Rivers at Rushmore was a glittering alliance and the high point of the family's fortunes. The prohibitive costs of parliamentary elections, the late 19th-century agricultural depression and poor management led to the break up of the Grove estates. Ironically, Sir Walter's eldest son was to spend his last days in Hollywood advising on the social life and culture of the English upper classes!

The medieval house at Ferne was replaced by a new one on the same site in 1811. This was much added to in the

19th century and again in 1903 by the Charlesworth family who stayed but a short time to lavish money on the house and adjoining village of Berwick St John.

The estate was then purchased in 1915 by Alfred Douglas-Hamilton, the invalid Duke of Hamilton and Brandon and his strong-minded wife, Nina. Vi Head, who remained active in Donhead St Andrew until her mid-nineties, came to work at Ferne in 1918. She recalled it with happy memories despite the long hours of work:

> I came to Ferne House at the age of seventeen from my home at Cholderton and stayed until I married five years later. My sister was there forty years from children's nurse to the Duchess's maid. I remember there were seven children. The youngest was Mairi, ('Star of the Sea'), Queen Mary's god daughter, who died whilst I was there following an accident. The Duchess would not allow certain treatments, much to the annoyance of the doctors and when Mairi died shortly afterwards she was buried in the grounds. Lord David, her brother, said they had little services on the lawn and that is where she would have liked to be buried rather than the family grave at Berwick St John.
>
> There was a large staff including four house maids and before I left I was the second. I was known as the dust hunter! There were twenty servants in the House alone including the four housemaids, four in the kitchen, four in the pantry, four in the laundry, plus gardeners and others outside.
>
> When Lord Fisher came I had to light his fire at 4.30 am – there was no central heating – 4.30 until after doing

Nina, Duchess of Hamilton and Brandon. With the Duke and their children she lived at Ferne. Here, during the 2nd World War she provided a home for animals, injured and homeless, as a result of the bombing. She also provided a home for as many as 50 children up to the age of five, when they were moved nearer to a school.

the beds at night about 9 pm, those were my hours. We had prayers every morning taken by the Duchess or one of the family.

Lord Fisher had been First Sea Lord after a distinguished naval career, and was a firm friend of the family. After the death of his wife, Fisher remained a permanent guest of the Hamilton's until his own death two years later.

As the interwar years passed, the duke's paralysis became more marked. He much admired his wife's work for animals and encouraged her involvement in the Animal

Staff with war refugee dogs at the animal refuge at Ferne. Nina, Duchess of Hamilton and Brandon, is on the right.

Defence and Antivivisection Society. The carnage of the First World War had affected them both. Shooting parties were never allowed on their property as the thought of killing for pleasure had become intolerable to them. After the duke's death at Ferne in 1940 the duchess lived there another eleven years to carry on a remarkable crusade.

At the commencement of war in 1939, the Animal Defence Society broadcast from London asking people in rural areas to give homes to evacuated animals. Although the London office was flooded with offers, there were not nearly sufficient for the vast numbers of distress calls that

Dogs leaving London for the animal refuge at Ferne. The animals were all from blitzed homes.

arrived. When the heavy bombing of London began, the work increased to a flood as the pets of service personnel and heavily committed workers were joined by the injured and homeless creatures of the blitz.

Many pets were put down. Other more fortunate ones including monkeys, parrots and domestic animals joined horses, donkeys and goats at Ferne which the duchess turned into an animal sanctuary. At times as many as one hundred and fifty dogs and one hundred and twenty cats had to be cared for before suitable homes could be found. The noise must have been deafening!

The Duchess's devotion to animals did not blind her to the greater need of bombed-out children. Throughout the war, Ferne provided a haven for many toddlers up to the age of five. At this stage accommodation had to be found for them nearer a school. There were up to fifty at a time with a war nursery managed by the Waifs and Strays (now the Church of England Children's Society).

After the war, Ferne Animal Sanctuary continued along improved lines, the estate remaining in the hands of the Animal Defence Society for many years after the duchess's death in 1951. In 1964 the house was demolished. All that remained until recently within this lovely parkland was a scattering of outhouses and a secluded grove – the final resting place for numerous pets and the grave of Mairi, the duchess's youngest daughter.

2

Semley
Unspoilt by Time

NORTH OF THE DONHEADS lies the village of Semley. Previously the possession of the Wilton Abbey estate from before the Norman conquest until the Dissolution, it was the only part of the old Chalke Hundred to lie within the Nadder Valley. Named after the River Sem which joins the Nadder near Wardour Castle, it lies on the formation of Kimmeridge clay that provides the extensive pasturage used mainly for dairying.

Village greens are not a noted feature of Wiltshire but at Semley we find one that is extensive and unspoiled. It is part of the 300 acres of common land scattered throughout the village. The fragmented nature of the common, some

opposite] An outing to Southsea by Semley villagers, 1939 – probably the last such event before the outbreak of war.

parts ill-drained and marshy, others fringing the lanes in long strips, explains its survival. Uneconomic to farm, inappropriate to enclose, it has provided a natural abode for wilder habitation and gives the village an air of spaciousness rarely experienced today even in rural societies.

Attempts to enclose or interfere with the common land have always been resisted fiercely. Until 1922 the use of the land by leaseholders to graze their cattle from May to November was regulated by the Manor Court. From that date onwards the twenty landowners and farmers with grazing rights appointed annually a 'Common Master' to oversee the strips and a 'Common Walker' to keep the land in good order. Unauthorised stock was removed and placed in the village pound next to the school.

Slate Club dinner at the Benett Arms, 1910. The landlady, Emily King, is standing in front in her clean apron. She is believed to have died about 1920 having fallen from one of the pub windows. Her daughter is standing in the doorway.

Until the mid-20th century there were gates across the Semley lanes to prevent straying from the common. By that time, however, increasing traffic was beginning to make the unfenced areas dangerous for straying cattle. In any case, most of the leaseholders, having attested herds, found the common grazing no longer of use. Today the grass is cut for hay and the common, protected by ancient statutes, remains for the enjoyment of all.

The hub of Semley life is Church Green. Here is to be found the Benett Arms, the blacksmith among scattered cottages and the mullion-windowed Church Farmhouse, a 17th-century reminder of the original settlements. The post office/general store has recently been closed, but the village school – a thriving community since 1841 – continues to prosper along the Donhead road at right angles to Church Green. It is along this road, steeply rising to Gutch Green,

William Sully the blacksmith at Semley who died in 1965. His wrought iron work can still be seen in many Semley gates and in the seat on Calais Hill.

above] A small statue in bronze (recently stolen) on a marble block in Semley churchyard. A creation of the sculptor Henry Pegram, it commemorates Lieut. George Armstrong who died at the family home in Semley in 1915.

right] Semley Home Guard practising with a selection of weapons at Foxholes above Gutch Common. Is that a German spy in the background?

that you will find the moss-covered Plague Stone nestling in foliage opposite the old Calais Cottages. It has a story reminiscent of the Derbyshire village of Eyam though less well documented. The stone had previously been the hollowed-out base of an ancient preaching cross situated in the centre of the village. When plague, presumably that of 1665, reached this area the residents on the higher ground of Gutch Common were apparently unaffected whilst those in lower-lying Semley suffered badly. Each day the inhabitants of Gutch Common filled the halfway stone with fresh water and left food beside it for their stricken neighbours who left coins in the water for payment.

St Leonard's lies to the south of Church Green, a small 'spirelet' surmounting the tower which is reputed to house one of the heaviest rings of six bells in the country. Built in 1874 by Thomas Wyatt, St Leonard's replaced an earlier Norman church of which only a circular Norman font and a 13th-century effigy of a priest remain.

Photograph of the old Semley church, which was gradually replaced by the present building from 1866. All that remains from this church is the circular Norman font and the 13th-century effigy of a priest, both close to the north door.

Of particular interest in the church is the variety of stained-glass windows ranging from 1866 to 1988. The most recent is that created by Henry Haig, the Dorset artist. It commemorates Yvonne Fletcher, whose home was in the village until she joined the 'Met' as a woman police officer. Whilst on duty outside the Libyan Embassy in St James's Square, London, she was shot and killed on 17 April 1984. The window reflects her love of the countryside and incorporates the badge of the Metropolitan Police.

Change came to Semley with the Salisbury to Yeovil Railway in 1859 (later to become the London & South Western Railway). A new road was built to the station from the main Shaftesbury to Warminster road and linked with the village centre. Around this artery a small industrial area developed with cottages for the workers and the Railway Hotel later to become the Kingsettle. As Semley was the

Yvonne Fletcher monument in St. James's Square, London

William and Sally Mallett, publicans of the Railway Hotel (subsequently the Kingsettle and now closed), with three of their six children, Winnie, Victor and Louisa, in the 1920s. A carpenter by trade, William also made coffins as well as being the village undertaker.

nearest station to Shaftesbury it is not surprising that a flourishing carrier trade soon grew up.

Mrs Louisa George whose parents, William and Sally Mallett, kept the inn remembers a life at the beginning of the 20th century that was often hectic but still left time for fun:

I came to the Railway Hotel when I was eighteen months old but my memories begin just after the War when I saw an Australian soldier coughing. A lot of people were ill because of the 'flu' epidemic which killed so many.

It was a homely, bustling pub, a focal point because of the station opposite. Apart from the bar work, mum and dad did quite a bit of catering: the Slate Club and the Pig Club, for instance, and the Conservative Club with the local MP at the head of the table. We cooked the food for functions in the hotel itself and rushed it across to the stable area which had been cleared of vehicles and the floor covered with sawdust.

My father had one of the first motor cars around, an old Ford T, and we had a van which was converted to take the children to school. Everyone, even Lord Arundell, came off the train to our pub so there was plenty of hire work as well. Father was a carpenter by trade and used to make coffins as well as being the undertaker. We also had a small-holding to maintain with pigs, chickens, cows and a donkey.

My mother was only forty-nine when she died which meant my father was left with six children under seventeen to bring up. We all had to help. Winnie had a band consisting of herself and four of her boyfriends. They played violin, drums and banjo with Winnie on the piano. They were called the Excelsior and played in the bar as well as for social occasions elsewhere.

The railway also led to the establishment of a milk distribution depot, the first in Wiltshire to serve the London market. Started in 1871 by Thomas Kirby adjacent to the Railway Hotel, it collected milk from the local farms. Its fortunes flourished under various ownerships but by the 1950s, with new state-of-the-art technology, milk was collected and cooled in the factory and carried by glass pipes over Station Road to specially designed, glass-lined rail tanks. With the closure of the station in the mid-sixties, however, Semley's industrial life diminished.

Joyce Johnson grew up in the isolated hamlet of Gutch Common which links Semley to the Donheads. Her memories indicate the toughness of rural life, especially for those affected by the Great war:

United Dairies depot and manager's house between the wars. The milk pipeline to the railway sidings at Semley station can be clearly seen.

Lorries at the United Dairies depot. Two Garner vehicles in the early 1920s (above left); Robert Woodrow standing by his open-sided cab (above right).

My family were farming people, connected with Gutch Common for generations, but Great Aunt Emily King kept the Benett Arms in Semley from the 1900s to 1920, a few years before I was born.

My father, Ebinezer Stone, came back from the First World War having lost both his legs in some of the heaviest fighting in the Gallipoli campaign. He was so ill that he had to stay with Aunt Emily at the Benett Arms because he couldn't cope on his own. With great courage and determination, he learnt to walk with a stick on artificial legs.

Ebenezer Stone with 'Old Bob' at his home at Gutch Common in 1933. Eby lost both is legs in the Gallipoli campaign.

His employment before the war had been as a groom at Stourton House, Stourhead, but that was obviously at an end. With a 100 per cent disability pension, he became a shoe repairer supplementing this by our smallholding. He also worked as a carrier taking people to the station in our pony and trap and bringing back fuel from the coal merchant there.

My mother had been his nurse during the war. They fell in love and married in 1920. Coming from Norwich, she found the existence of a small community hard to bear. I remember her trimming the oil lamps and cleaning the lampshade with a cloth and stick or fetching water from the well at the bottom of the Stickle Path. But I was rarely lonely. I fed the pigs and chickens on our small plot and loved to brush and comb our old pony Bob. Often I would open the common gates for motor cars in the hope of a penny or halfpenny. Each afternoon the wagon would pass taking watercress to Semley Station and Ernest Coward would deliver milk from a can which he poured with great care into mother's waiting jug.

Despite its closeness to Shaftesbury, Semley has retained its air of rustic tranquillity. The old railway complex, however, has seen a resurgence of commercial and industrial activity. Light engineering units, an auction house and a garden centre are among those bringing fresh opportunity and a sense of balance to this pleasant agricultural community.

3

Burgus Hindon

H INDON, with its handsome tree-lined street rising from the Dene to the church and beyond, is a gem of 18th-century architecture, its fine Chilmark stone houses rising like a phoenix from the ashes of the terrible fire it endured in 1754. It is also a community of local historians and I am indebted to Norah Sheard and

Looking up Hindon High Street from the Dene in 1863

Richard Dewhurst whose own authoritative works on the history of Hindon were themselves gleaned from the investigations of earlier researchers.

Before 1219 the area was little more than open downland populated by sheep, but a convergence of ancient trackways to the north may have influenced the landlords – the bishops of Winchester – in their decision to build a new borough here. A shrewd decision. Hindon's position, suitably distanced from the surrounding markets of Salisbury, Shaftesbury and Mere and along the Salisbury to Taunton route must have suggested the possibility of future prosperity.

So it was that Bishop des Roches from 1219 to 1220 'planted' the new town of Burgus Hindon in the manor of East Knoyle. Its success was rapid for by mid-century there were one hundred and fifty houses situated on either side of the main street bringing rents to the bishopric. Each house with a long narrow garden ended at a back lane for access to the fields. That on the west side is still in use as a footpath after seven hundred years.

By mid-century, a weekly market had been granted by royal assent and later augmented by yearly or bi-annual fairs. The market cross, an important symbol of a market town, stood near the present day post office until the 19th century. The town prospered and by 1650 John Aubrey, the Wiltshire historian, considered the market as second only to Warminster as the largest corn market in southern England.

Hindon's prosperity continued unabated until the mid-18th century, its bustling community servicing the

above] John Martin the thatcher of Hindon, who died in 1924 aged 93, with his wife Rhoda who was a founder member of the Methodist chapel

right] Hindon School children in about 1930 with their schoolmistress Miss V Andrews

productive villages of the Nadder and Wylye Valleys, its position on the Salisbury to Taunton road ensuring a constant demand for accommodation from passing travellers. Milestones within a wide radius pointed the way to Hindon and as many as fourteen inns were recorded there.

On 2 July 1754, at around three in the afternoon, Hindon received a dramatic blow to its fortunes. A spark from the forge of Mr Tyler, a cutler, ignited the thatch of his house on the western side of the High Street above the church. The houses were mostly constructed of brick and timber or flint with wattle and daub, each with a topping of thatch. Not surprisingly, with a high wind blowing, the flames spread rapidly from one side of the street to the other. Having been built on high ground the town wells were deep, making water for fire-fighting difficult to obtain.

By the evening one hundred and forty houses were burned to the ground as well as numerous barns and stables. All the inns were destroyed save one and a vast quantity of hay, corn and beer had perished. It is a wonder that only one of the inhabitants was killed. Within four hours the accomplishment of five centuries was seriously damaged, though contemporary accounts that the whole town was destroyed appear to have been exaggerated.

The disaster brought a sympathetic response from a wide area with relief funds set up as far away as Canterbury. Although Hindon rebuilt its fine houses with stone from the Tisbury and Chilmark quarries, the market declined and its prosperous economic base began to founder. Fortunately a new epoch was about to begin for which Hindon, straddling the main road to the west, was ideally situated.

opposite] Rawlings's drapery and general store early last century. Today the building is occupied by the Swan Gallery. May Gray worked here for 25 years from the age of 14 and brought up his two sons. 'He was one of the best drapers for miles around but you ought to have seen the beautiful tea services he broke up when he was angry!' The photograph shows (left to right): Miss Rose (later Mrs Rawlings), Miss Bees, Jim Beckett, Mr Rawlings, Mr Roberts, Mr Burt.

Increasing trade between London and the south-west led to the gradual improvement of arterial roads. Turnpike trusts, with parliamentary powers, erected gates and extracted tolls to bring about the necessary improvements. The first London-Exeter mail coach passed through Hindon on 2 August 1784. The great coaching era had begun. Hindon was well placed to take full advantage of the passing traffic. New inns were built, six of them around the main highway. The Crown, now the post office, brewed its own beer and had stabling at the rear. The Lamb, with the Angel (also known as the Grosvenor), the only ones to remain, kept as many as three hundred post horses in the surrounding fields. Others, now converted to houses, can still be recognised by their arched entrances and cobbled yards.

Less pleasing in Hindon's history was its political reputation. Camden, in Elizabethan times, described it as

Three genteel ladies, Mrs Vic Read, Mrs J Ranger and Mrs G Cheverall take tea in a Hindon garden early last century

left] Cottages at the upper end of Hindon High Street, beyond the church, in 1909. Included in the photograph are Mr J Beckett, Mrs M Gray, Mrs Newberry and Miss Stanton.

'one of the rottenest of the rotten boroughs'. Corruption, bribery and mob violence were rife at that time but the Hindon burgers continued during the ensuing centuries to elect their two members of Parliament by ruthlessly manipulating the various bidders.

The Reform Act of 1832 concluded Hindon's days as a rotten borough signalling the gradual decline of its

right] Maypole dancing at Hindon School, c. 1918, with the headteacher, Mr Lang, and the vicar, the Revd Lumsden. May Gray describes the school at that time as 'cold, filthy and lousy – we had to have our hair tied back'. She was there from the age of three.

left] Boys enjoying (or enduring) a digging lesson outside Hindon School house, 1933-4. Notice the uniformity of action still expected at that time.

prosperity. Two years earlier the Swing Riots, highlighting the poverty and discontent of the rural working class, had disrupted the Hindon market. When the mob passed through on its way to Tisbury it broke up the agricultural machines brought for sale and exhibition. As the 19th century progressed, the spread of the railways throughout England was bringing to an end the age of coaching. With the building of the Salisbury-Yeovil line in 1859, its nearest station three miles away at Tisbury, Hindon dwindled into the small village it is now.

W H Hudson, the famous writer and naturalist, was a frequent visitor to Hindon at the beginning of the 20th century. A tall, lean figure, he would often be seen touring the area on his heavy Sunbeam bicycle or striding the heights of Great Ridge Wood where he records observing with joy a young roebuck flashing through the trees. In 1909 he spent

several weeks at the Lamb where he described the gradual rearing of a family of flycatchers who remained unperturbed by the noisy activity of the inn.

Basil Bevis traces his family back through four generations of Hindon life. His great grandfather, George Bevis, was a tailor when one suit of tough broadcloth lasted from manhood to old age. His grandfather, William, was a master builder involved with the building of the new church in 1871. The previous building had been a chapel-of-ease to the mother church at East Knoyle where couples had to go to be married. As the journey was well over a mile across the hills they had plenty of opportunity to change their minds! William Bevis had twelve children who gradually moved away from the village with the necessity to find work. Only Basil's father remained at Hindon where the close neighbourliness of village life helped the residents through hard times:

> Everybody helped one another. There was not all that much money around. I was always working for someone else to help my father's debts. People were never really hard up because

left] Hindon's old chapel of ease before it was taken down around 1869 and replaced by the present church on the same site in 1870. Next door is seen the home of George Snook, plumber and village carrier, which was also demolished. The shop to its right is the present village store and post office (previously the Crown Inn).

everyone had a pig; you can get a lot from that and then you could always pick up a rabbit or two. You grew all the vegetables you wanted, there was always turnips and swedes in the fields. Everyone had an apple or plum tree. If you did not have one a friend usually did.

By the time of the First World War, Hindon had long since passed its heyday as a borough. Its bustling market, its annual fairs and the prosperity of the coaching era had passed into history. Both the petty sessions court and police station had moved to Tisbury. The war was to bring further change and Basil Bevis recalls some of the immediate effects it had on Hindon life:

> I suppose my most vivid memories are of the 1914 war. I remember going to Pythouse Park on a hot August Sunday evening to wish the Old Contemptibles goodbye before they entrained at Tisbury station for France.

right] The former petty sessions court and police station at the lower end of Hindon High Street.

On one occasion I saw an Australian soldier at the bridge, sitting on the side of the road having a meal. He had a good view each way. We had a chat and he asked about the wood. I formed the opinion he was a deserter. We often saw the military police taking men back to camp. They rode horses and the men were handcuffed to the stirrup.

The early aircraft were just starting and we had several land on the downs. They came from Old Sarum. Once in the air they got their direction from landmarks so they often got lost. It only needed a heavy rain storm to force them down. They would then commandeer any soldier handy to mount guard over their plane whilst they went back to camp.

Hay and straw were in great demand for the war effort. I remember my uncles who had a farm in the village selling a large haystack. The RASC came along with a bailer to get it ready for hauling to Tisbury station. This was done by horse transport. All the stabling at the Lamb Inn and the Grosvenor Arms was taken over by the army. The Abbey Woods had some good stands of timber so the Canadian lumberjacks came and got busy. The saw mill was at Stone Gate. The timber was then taken to Tisbury by steam tractor.

Until the 1920s Hindon had changed little in appearance. Its nine oil lamps, a symbol of earlier munificence, still lit the High Street although the old inns, apart from the Grosvenor and Lamb, had already been sub-divided into houses and shops. As the years passed, new

A wagon load of baskets made by John Beckett of Hindon, who is standing at the horse's head

Hindon

Unveiling the war memorial in Hindon High Street by Hugh Morrison MP, 17 October 1919. The vicar is the Revd Lumsden. In 1943 the memorial was partly demolished by an American tank and later rebuilt by the church. Hindon post office lies in the background.

agricultural methods and modern transport brought fresh changes. The downs were ploughed up and fenced. No longer would sheep pass like a tide from nearby Berwick St Leonard to pasture on Hindon Down. Between the wars a steady increase in traffic brought renewed vigour to the Hindon roads. So much so that when an American tank knocked down the war memorial in 1943 it was moved to a less intrusive spot alongside the church.

Today, Hindon retains its air of past grandeur. The broad tree-lined pavements of the High Street fronting elegant Georgian residences remind us that it was once more than a village. Expansion and modernisation have inevitably changed its character but Hudson would still have found it 'contented and merry and exhibiting a sweet friendliness towards the stranger'.

4

The Fonthills

Beckford's Glittering Folly

*Architecture at Fonthill is catastrophic, and houses there tend to
live adventurous lives.*

Edith Olivier

C LOSELY ALLIED to the fortunes of Hindon are those
of its southern neighbour, Fonthill Park. Here
William Beckford converted a treeless plateau,
some 250 ft higher than the cathedral at Salisbury, into 'a
flowering wilderness' and placed within it a Gothic abbey of
heroic proportions. So much has been written about this
colourful eccentric but the facts of his Fonthill involvement
lose nothing in the re-telling.

The 'Pavilion' at Fonthill Park, c. 1900. This was the remaining part of Alderman Beckford's Fonthill Splendens, after the rest had been plundered by his son. The Pavilion was the home of the Morrison family, but was demolished in 1922.

opposite] William Beckford junior, aged 21, painting by George Romney

Beckford's father, alderman and twice Lord Mayor of London, had inherited his immense wealth from sugar plantations in Jamaica. Though susceptible to violent bouts of temper, he was intelligent and cultured. He purchased Fonthill around 1736, determined to stamp his own identity on the estate with its Elizabethan mansion which had been re-faced in the classical style. When a dramatic fire destroyed much of his new home he replaced it with a Palladian residence of great splendour.

Fonthill Splendens, for such was it known, was situated at the bottom of a wooded valley. It was approached through the magnificent classical archway which still stands on the northern edge of the estate. The arch was probably created by him at the same time as the artificial lake with its bridge, grotto and elegant boathouse. A classical church, temple and pagoda also believed to have been built under his direction, have long since disappeared.

left] The old saw mills at
Fonthill Gifford during the 1st
World War

below] Thomas Coombs and
his niece Miss Applin. Both
served as Fonthill Bishop
churchwardens, he from 1887
to 1893, she from 1921 to
1946.

Alderman Beckford was not to enjoy this opulence
long, for he died in 1770 leaving his ten-year-old son,
William Beckford junior, to enjoy the estate. William
inherited a fortune of £100,000 per year as well as his
father's violent temper and quixotic nature. A brilliant
linguist, he also claimed to have studied art and architecture
at the feet of the greatest exponents of his day and music
with the young Mozart. At the age of twenty he wrote
Vathek, an oriental novel regarded as unique in Western
literature, as well as travelogues of his subsequent tours of
Europe. He loved animals and, although riding was his
lifelong pursuit, he would allow no hunting on his land.

It was in 1793 that Beckford gave serious thought to
his vision of a Gothic ruin, then so fashionable. His was to
be on a vaster scale than any other attempted. He selected
James Wyatt, one of the most celebrated architects of his

opposite left] The sheepwash
at Fonthill Bishop in 1907

opposite right] Haymaking at
Fonthill Park early in the 20th
century

time, for this purpose. The site he chose was Hinkley Hill situated in the north-western portion of his estate. To ensure privacy he enclosed 519 acres with a wall 12 ft high and 3½ miles long. It had metal spikes along the top and six locked gateways. Within these walls an estimated one million trees were planted to surround the abbey, intermingled in planned confusion. An American plantation led to an enlarged ornamental lake. This exotic landscape is thought to have inspired the poet Coleridge in his vision of Kubla Khan:

> So twice five miles of fertile ground
> With walls and towers were girdled round:
> And there were gardens bright with sinuous rills,
> Where blossomed many an incense-bearing tree;

The creation of the abbey itself proceeded less successfully. Beckford's impatience to see the work done did not blend well with Wyatt's unreliability. The huge central tower which was to be the jewel of his abbey was flimsily constructed and collapsed in a strong wind. Undeterred, Beckford ordered a replacement, this time encased in stone which rose to a commanding height of 250 ft. Throughout the summer of 1800 work continued at a feverish pace. Five hundred men with every wagon in the district worked shifts day and night while local farmers grumbled secretively about their diminished labour force.

To complete his plans, Beckford was forced by his need for stone to demolish a major part of his father's house, Fonthill Splendens. The new building was to consist of four

The Lancaster Tower, the remaining section of William Beckford's Fonthill Abbey, seen in the early 1900s. The rest collapsed in 1825.

wings spreading in a cross from the central octagon which was to be surmounted by a tower. By 1802 this massive structure was sufficiently complete for Beckford to take up residence. But the costs of this venture, furnished with pictures and other works of art of great value, extended even his vast income. As Beckford's affairs reached a crisis in 1822 he sold the estate in its entirety to a Scottish millionaire, John Farquhar, and retired to fresh enterprises at Bath.

Beckford's involvement with Fonthill might then have ended had not a dying man, the contractor employed by Wyatt, requested an urgent visit. He confessed to Beckford that the foundations of the central tower had not been laid according to the agreed specifications and were faulty. Beckford immediately informed Farquhar of this and the possible danger of the tower falling, a warning Farquhar chose to ignore. On 21 December 1825, the tower collapsed destroying much of the abbey but fortunately injuring no one. An immense cloud of dust darkened the sky for miles around, announcing to the world that Beckford's grand project was, with the exception of the small fragment remaining today, at an end.

~ ~ ~

By the 1830s, the Fonthill estate had been broken into two. The western portion, including the abbey ruins, was acquired by the 2nd Earl Grosvenor, soon to become the Marquis of Westminster. In 1860 he built a new abbey in Scottish baronial style south of the old abbey ruins. It is also notable that he built three of the Nadder Valley churches, those of Semley, Hindon and Fonthill Gifford. In 1879, after

After the 1830s the Fonthill Estate was broken into two. The abbey ruins were purchased by the Marquis of Westminster who built a new 'abbey' in 1860 in the Scottish baronial style. It was demolished after the 2nd World War.

his death, his daughter Lady Octavia and her husband Sir Michael Shaw-Stewart moved into the house. It remained with them and their descendants until requisitioned by the army in 1940. After the war its structure was found to be faulty and it was demolished in 1955 to the consternation of local villagers who thought the war had started all over again!

The eastern part of Beckford's estate, including the remaining portion of Fonthill Splendens, passed to the Morrison family. James Morrison, born in Hampshire in 1790, started his career in the modest role of a London warehouseman. His evident ability, however, led to a partnership in the drapery business of Joseph Todd whose

right] The previous home of the Morrison family at Little Ridge, Fonthill Park. The wing on the right is Old King's House which was previously a derelict manor house transferred from Berwick St Leonard by Hugh Morrison. This was replaced in 1972 by the present residence at Little Ridge.

The lavishly furnished interior of Fonthill House, known as 'The Pavilion', c. 1885

daughter he married. James was a pioneer in the field of 'small profits, quick returns' and by the age of thirty-three had made a considerable fortune. He invested his money in land, notably at Fonthill Park.

After his death in 1857, Alfred, his second son, enriched the house with numerous works of art including many masterpieces especially made for him by eminent craftsmen. His son, Hugh, who inherited in 1897, devoted his energies to politics, representing Salisbury as its MP for long periods. The stylishly transformed Fonthill Splendens known as The Pavilion was not to his taste and, taking advantage of a fire early in the 20th century, he abandoned it to build a fresh property. This he did by removing the derelict Elizabethan manor house from the estate village of Berwick St Leonard and replacing it stone by stone at Little Ridge to the eastern end of the park.

After Hugh Morrison's death in 1941, the estate continued in the possession of his son John. He also served as Salisbury's MP continuously from 1942 until his elevation to the peerage in 1964 as Baron Margadale of Islay. In 1972 he had the restored Berwick manor house demolished yet again and the present, much smaller, mansion built on the same site – the last of a confusing number of Fonthill dwellings.

Of the three Fonthill villages, it is Berwick St Leonard, today the smallest and least known, which might claim the greatest historical significance. When Prince William of Orange, on his fateful journey from Torbay to London, met Lord Clarendon for urgent consultations in December 1688, the venue had been the Lamb at Hindon but it was Berwick Manor where he lodged. Here he prepared himself for the final journey to London the next day to claim his throne. By 1900 this mansion, now an ivy-clad ruin, had declined to a chicken house before its brief restoration as the home of the Morrisons at Little Ridge.

Berwick St Leonard deserves recognition for its importance as the site of an ancient sheep fair. Many such gatherings were held at strategic points on hills or downland near the old trackways leading to London. Cold Berwick Hill, a windy and exposed area, was admirably suited for this purpose and a fair was held there over many centuries always on St Leonard's Day, 6 November. Bonfires were lit to guide drovers along the ancient tracks from the western counties and horse dealers who travelled from Ireland. Here, there was sufficient space for the standing booths, sheep coops and horse ties needed. Here, too, the publicans of Hindon could bring their cartloads of beer to refresh the mingling crowds who arrived to trade or to enjoy the excitement of such an occasion.

Reg Harris, who worked on the estate all his life, loved the activities of the Irish horse traders. What fascinated him was to get behind the scenes and watch them prepare an old nag for sale by putting a piece of ginger under its tail. The burning sensation made it cock up its tail and trot round the ring like a two-year-old with the Irish dealer hoping to make a quick sale before the effect wore off.

Changes in trading methods accompanying the Industrial Revolution helped to diminish the importance of local fairs. The railways, too, made it easier to transport sheep

A 19th-century painting of Berwick Hill fair house now long since demolished. Fairs were held on St Leonard's Day, 6 November. When the hurdles had been removed for use at the fair, the house was used by the Hindon publicans as a refreshment centre.

over long distances and cheaper imported lamb reduced the profitability of the home-grown variety. Certainly by 1910 the once great fair of Berwick St Leonard had ceased to be mentioned in local records.

Neighbouring Fonthill Bishop straddles the old London to Taunton road but had only one inn to compete

Harvest at Fonthill Park with land girls and German prisoners of war, c. 1916

with Hindon. Its centre nestles tightly around the now defunct school and the Early English St Leonard's Church. Dr Wren, father of the famous architect Sir Christopher Wren, was rector here in 1620. During his brief incumbency he married the daughter of a churchwarden and later moved to East Knoyle where Christopher was born.

On the opposite side of the road lies the magnificent Palladian archway. It is difficult to pass through and enjoy this lovely park without a sense of intrusion. At the far end lies Fonthill Gifford at the very centre of the divided estates and shrouded in woodland like an alpine village. From here the road runs southwards from the genteel retirement of the old borough of Hindon to its enterprising neighbour, Tisbury.

The Fonthill Arch built in the mid-18th century for Alderman William Beckford as the entrance gate ot Fonthill Park

Fonthill Gifford Peace Pageant following the 1st World War

5
Tisbury
Centre of the Western
Nadder

TISBURY IS A PERFECT EXAMPLE of the old country adage, 'if you are going to such-and-such you shouldn't be starting from 'ere!' Situated between the main arterial roads, the A303 and the A30, it has no major road passing through it and, therefore, would not be visited without good reason. Proudly aware of its status as a large active village rather than a small town, it is no modern upstart milking the previous wealth of Hindon but is one of the oldest communities in Wiltshire with roots that precede the monastic establishment of Shaftesbury.

The original inhabitants may well have lived east of the village at the hilltop fortress now known as Castle Ditches. It would have been so much easier to protect than the marshy valley below where the Nadder continues its tortuous route to Wilton. Tysse's Burgh, however, meaning 'the stronghold of Tysse's people', was the Saxon name for the later riverside settlement they developed between the 6th and 11th centuries. Many of the settlements that evolved then, including Bridzor, Hatch and Wick, retain their names today. Reference to an abbot of Tisbury in the 8th century indicates the existence of a monastery of note, but this had disappeared by 888 when the whole of the Tisbury estate was granted to King Alfred's new abbey at Shaftesbury.

The present parish church of St John, flanking the northern bank of the Nadder, dates from the late 12th century but has been much added to by ensuing generations. It is a fine cruciform building whose central tower has had an unfortunate history. On Midsummer Eve 1742 the spire was struck by lightning. Twenty years later during a violent storm, it was struck again, this time crashing down through the central structure. Following this the spire was replaced by a second storey, giving the tower, with its ring of six bells, the appearance we see today.

St John's is exceptionally large for a village church and contains much of interest. Its lofty nave has a 15th-century wagon roof with angel heads peeping down and 16th-century panelled ceilings adorning the aisles. Above the northern porch entrance is a stone chamber used once by

Return of Tisbury church bells after re-tuning in 1926. Florrie Rayson is wearing the cloche hat and Mr John Freeman, the headmaster, is centre holding a cigarette.

'Punch' (centre) and 'Josh' (right) working in the grounds of Tisbury workhouse, Monmouth Hill, early 20th century. Tisbury parish church is in the background.

chantry priests and reputedly at one time the chilly home of a local hermit. The 'Beggar's Porch' at the western end has a rather squashed look, being originally 3 ft higher. It was reduced during the 19th century in order to lengthen the window after the removal of the old gallery.

Within the churchyard stands a yew tree reputedly well over a thousand years old and now disfigured by a massive concrete interior. The ancient market cross, once lodged at the top of the High Street, adjoins the recently-established Garden of Remembrance. At the chancel end lie the graves of Rudyard Kipling's parents who lived in Hindon Lane. John Lockwood Kipling was eminent in his own right as a skilled sculptor and as one of the illustrators of his son's books.

One earlier Tisbury resident not to be buried in the churchyard was Thomas Mayhew. Born in 1593, his family had already been associated with the close-knit Nadder Valley communities for centuries but he was to make his fortune in the New World. With a legacy from his father he became apprenticed to a mercer in Southampton and at twenty-one was able as 'a free commoner' to set up on his own. His dealings with vessels from New England may well have stimulated his wish to settle there – the *Mayflower*, for example, sailed from Southampton during his first year of trading. Eventually he accepted the post of agent in Massachusetts to a wealthy London merchant and arrived in 1631 with his wife and ten-year-old son, Thomas junior.

As his fortunes prospered, Thomas Mayhew was able to take over part of his employer's business and purchase the offshore islands of Martha's Vineyard and Nantucket.

View looking from the Square up Tisbury High Street towards the Benett Arms, with the post office in the angle of roads to the right, 1st World War

At a place now called Edgartown on Martha's Vineyard, his son became pastor, the first of several generations of 'Missionary Mayhews'. They helped establish the townships of Tisbury and Chilmark and ministered to the spiritual needs of the Indian population as well as the settlers. Thomas Mayhew senior lived to be eighty-eight, following his son, who tragically died at sea, as Governor of Martha's Vineyard. In 1977 descendants of the family returned on a visit to Tisbury, England, re-establishing bonds between the two communities.

Fringing St John's churchyard at its western end are the imposing 17th-century stone and brick almshouses bearing the Biblical text 'As for me and my house we will serve the Lord'. Here, on a bend of the Nadder known as Stubbles, you will find the old National school. After its closure it was donated to the village by Lord Hinton of

left] Hibberd's Emporium in Tisbury High Street, c. 1907

The outer gateway to Place Farm, seen from the river, with the tithe barn behind it to the right, and farmhouse and courtyard to the left. Members of the Strong family are shown by the river.

Bankside in memory of his father who had been headmaster at the beginning of the 20th century. Now known as Hinton Hall at his request, it continues to serve the village as a religious and cultural centre.

The magnificent outer gateway of Place Farm stands sentinel at the eastern end of the village and should not be missed. It has two imposing gatehouses, the outer one with two entrances: one to admit a loaded wagon, the other suitably shaped for a horse and rider. Although until recently a working farm on the Fonthill Estate, it has an air of sleepy retirement belying its medieval importance. Built for the Abbess of Shaftesbury in the 14th and 15th centuries, it incorporated large and elaborate buildings for residence, worship, agriculture and tithe collection. For the latter purpose, the farmyard contains the largest barn in England, 188 ft long and 32 ft wide, a vast structure of local stone with thirteen bays and imposing transeptal entrances. The roof, originally covered with stone tiles, is now thatched.

One cannot wander far from Place Farm without being aware of the presence of water. Both Fonthill and Ansty Brooks join the Nadder near here. Kingfishers nest along the narrow causeway which links the farm to a picturesque mill whose history pre-dates Domesday. The late Captain S J Parker recorded memories of his youth here as the miller's son:

> The mill was in full production at the turn of the century when most villagers had a pig in the sty and the farmers obtained their feeding stuff from the mill for their cattle. After heavy rains there was usually too much water to work the mill, and the surplus was diverted from the main stream by four hatches which, when raised, sent a rush of

The Bartlett family outside Tisbury mill in about 1903. Letitia Bartlett is seated in the centre, with her sons Herbert (standing 2nd left), James and Charles (standing, right) and their families.

water into a deep pool that to us seemed to be hundreds of feet deep. The water from two of the hatches passed through an iron cage which caught many fish, sometimes weighing 12 or 14 lbs which we collected when the floods had subsided.

Following an injury in 1919, the elderly Mr Parker was forced to leave. Two years later the mill was converted by a private company to supply electricity to the village until taken over by the Wessex Electricity Company in 1930.

The brewery is in Church Street, a grim reminder of earlier days when the abject poverty of rural Wiltshire was felt here as keenly as anywhere. A workhouse existed on this site as early as 1769 and for a parish of fewer than two thousand, the number and cost of the poor were high. The post-Napoleonic depression and the Poor Law Amendment Act of 1834, which abolished outdoor relief, swelled its numbers still further. A report of the Commissioners for Lunacy in 1862 found the building to be in a state of extreme dilapidation. Barely furnished and cheerless rooms swarmed with rats, mice and bugs, with water running down the walls in winter. The inmates were separated according to sex but old and young, good and bad, were herded together in these squalid conditions. Only two privies existed, contaminated by seepage from the adjacent burial ground. Sandwiched between the graveyard and the mortuary, it is no wonder that it was known locally as 'the dead house'!

Although poverty continued to be evident until well into the last century, the creation of the Salisbury-Yeovil railway in 1859, with its station at Tisbury, brought new prosperity transforming the village into the shape we see today. A speculator from Hindon, Archibald Beckett, took out a lease on the area known as Paradise Field in the centre of the village. Clearly the narrow hollow through which Tisbury High Street wended its way to the new station was totally impracticable for the increasing traffic. This, Beckett bypassed with a broader, more direct route flanked with new shops and houses. They blend well with older properties – apart from the Benett Arms which seems more in keeping with the Boscombe Arcade he built later at Bournemouth.

Tisbury

right] An early 20th century view of Tisbury, far less built up than now, with the busy railway station in the foreground

below] The Workhouse on Monmouth Hill, Tisbury, was built in 1868 to replace an older workhouse by the church. It was demolished in the late 1960s.

Brewery workers at Styringe's Brewery, as it was known in the early 20th century

When a new workhouse was built at Monmouth Hill in 1868, Beckett constructed the brewery on the site of the old one. This burnt down in 1885 but, undeterred, he built it up again with his name proudly engraved above the front entrance. Two new roads from the east, Park Road and The

Revd F E Hutchinson (vicar 1858-1913) shown outside his massive vicarage

Avenue, were provided by local landowners. These supplemented the steep incline of Cuffs Lane, thus completing the framework upon which modern Tisbury has developed.

Spanning this period of economic awakening was the Rev. F E Hutchinson, Vicar of Tisbury from 1858 to 1913, a man of surprising athleticism. Mrs Emily Miles, headmistress of the infants' school at the beginning of the 20th century and Tisbury's first local historian, records him jumping hurdles in the High Street to the great astonishment of bystanders. On another occasion he refused a lift home from Salisbury in the carrier's cart as he was in a hurry and preferred to run the distance! His wife, too, enjoyed outdoor exercise, riding a good deal to hounds and taking on fences and ditches that other riders preferred to avoid. Despite this behaviour, so uncharacteristic of Victorian clerics, their influence on the area was immense. Generous to a fault, their considerable wealth was used lavishly to improve the fabric of the church, the schools and on parish life in general.

Nonconformist groups had met in and around Tisbury since the 1660s but it was not until 1726 that sufficient unity led to the establishment of its first chapel. A substantial square building surmounted by a weathercock and with a fine internal gallery, it can still be viewed in ivy-clad isolation peeping from behind houses opposite the Boot Inn. This Presbyterian foundation was traditionally believed to have been built by quarrymen from Chilmark who laboured on it by night and left their womenfolk to guard it daily against the intrusions of bigoted opponents.

By the early 19th century, it was clear that a larger centre of worship was needed but it was not until 1842 that an imposing new chapel was opened at Zion Hill. Described by Betjeman as 'the Non-Conformists' answer to the Establishment's Gothic', it was built on solid rock and towers above the village at its eastern side. First to preach there was William Jay. He was born in humble circumstances in a small cottage in Tisbury Row, a worshipper in the old chapel as a boy, and had risen to be one of the most sought-after preachers of his day.

In 1976 lightning toppled the front main pinnacle of Zion Hill Chapel. Although this was repaired, further serious faults were discovered in its structure. Reluctantly, it was closed and its congregation joined with the Methodists worshipping in the High Street. Until recently, Zion Hill Chapel presented a sad spectacle. Standing amidst the leaning tomb-stones of dissenting families, its shuttered windows facing across the Nadder to the railway it awaited, like its predecessor opposite the Boot Inn, a final resolution of its fate. Today both have commenced a new existence having been converted into residential accommodation.

~ ~ ~

One among many colourful families to bridge the last three centuries of Tisbury life was the Osmonds. Thomas, the elder, was a patriarchal figure. He constructed the clock on the new tower of St John's Church in 1795 which continued to strike until replaced by the present three-dial one in 1927. An ardent churchman, he once rang a peal of bells in the belfry with six of his seven sons. His grave near the old yew tree in the churchyard marks his great skill as a clock and watch maker. Carved on the upper part of the stone is a clockface with the words 'My time is in thy Hands' carved around the dial.

The eldest son of this long-lived family was another Thomas who continued the clock-making trade. He was particularly famous for his grandfather clocks, one of which remained until recently in the hall of Clock House, the home he built for himself on the corner of The Avenue. His initials and the date 1828 can be seen engraved on the entrance.

While Thomas junior continued the family business, two of his brothers gained eminence in the field of monumental masonry. William, encouraged by the architect Pugin, designed and carved many of the Gothic memorials in Salisbury Cathedral. His own memorial can be seen on the wall of the cloisters. Joseph Osmond worked on Beckford's abbey at Fonthill as well as on many of the great buildings, symbols of Victorian prosperity, rising in the capital. These included the new Houses of Parliament in connection with which he made many journeys by sea to the Portland quarries in order to check the quality of the stone.

Youngest son of this family was George. As a boy he was already showing something of the mechanical skills possessed by his family. Emily Miles records an amusing occasion when he displayed this to the vicar's displeasure:

The coat-of-arms hung on the wall of the tower inside the Church, in front of the small belfry window above the pulpit. Unknown to anyone he painted out the lion's paw, affixed a false paw, made of tin, attached to it a wire which he carried through the window and connected it with the works of the clock. The following Sunday, while the sermon was being preached, the clock struck twelve, and the lion's paw moved up and down with the strokes of the hour. All eyes were fixed on the coat-of-arms, and the Vicar said, 'Either I must stop preaching, or Thomas Osmond must stop the clock!'

Tisbury, like its neighbour Chilmark, has always been noted for its working of the local Purbeck limestone. Evidence of such activity is widespread from the private quarry of the Fonthill estate – used for a succession of

Tom Lilley's stoneyard near Tisbury station early in the 20th century, from where stone from Chilmark and Tisbury quarries was shipped. Mr Gething, the Chilmark quarry owner, is in front with trilby hat. Several members of the Rixon family are present in the group.

aristocratic residences – to the open-cast excavations at Chicksgrove still producing fine quality stone today.

The Rixons were stone masons for generations. The 1881 Census, for example, shows James Rixon and his wife Isobella bringing up a family of nine children in the tiny Zion Hill cottage that clings to the rock below the chapel. Around the village can be seen grotesque carved heads, said to represent local characters, which he sculpted from the local stone. A range of these adorned his own cottage until the 1930s when an unthinking gardener ripped the ivy off and the heads, becoming detached, rolled away down the steep hill.

Despite the changes brought by the railway, Tisbury's subsequent fortunes have been mixed. Ralph Jackson, the most diligent of all local historians, came to the village in 1927 as branch manager of SCATS. His description of life at that period was not a happy one:

Zion Hill Cottage. Rebecca Dicker, daughter of James Rixon the stonemason, is standing in the doorway with her son Charlie. Notice the many heads carved by James Rixon, who had lived there previously with his wife Isobella and ten children.

This was a time of depression for farming, and many necessary farm jobs were reduced or stopped altogether. Hedges were untrimmed, ditches uncleaned, buildings deteriorated. The general dilapidation was not confined to farms however. Many houses and cottages remained unpainted and unrepaired. The churchyard also became uncared for with the grass growing more than knee-high. People were very hard up. Unemployment was high with more than 100 out-of-work persons registered at the Tisbury Labour Exchange.

Kathleen Mould, whose book *Reflections* charts her long life in the village, gives a personal view of the poverty of that period:

Times were hard after the Great War. We were living at Hindon in Jubilee Buildings and my father was trying to build up the old business – chimney sweeping (chimneys being very much in the fashion then).

One day he went about 5 am to sweep a few chimneys at 6d each, hoping to earn 3s 11d to buy Mum a pair of gloves to push my sister and me into Tisbury. On his way back he called into Grandma's. When she said 'Come on in, my son, we've just killed the pig', Dad replied, 'I can't eat it as Gladys and the children are starving.' Hence our coming to live with Grandma Strong at Court Street, Tisbury and Dad being forced to join the Royal Navy.

Tisbury has continued to reflect the fortunes and misfortunes of rural life, proving a successful breeding ground for many small businesses. Toby Baker, for example, was nearly 95 when he died in the year 2000. He was born in the butcher's shop halfway up the High Street (now the chemist's). It was originally started by his grandfather. Prize cattle would be purchased from Salisbury Market to be despatched by Toby and his helper, Billy Jay, in the slaughter house opposite the shop. For 5s he would buy a churn of tar from the old Tisbury Gas Works to kill off the numerous rats that plagued them.

George Maidment and Charlie Hull took advantage of the new tarmac roads to develop thriving transport businesses. Beckett's imposing brewery has been home to a number of trades including printing, woodworking and the production of animal feed before returning to the manufacture of beer. It has now been converted into private accommodation.

In 1890 the firm of P J Parmiter and Son, with its four employees, moved from Wardour to a small hut by the railway. Phillip Parmiter had previously developed the flexible chain harrow for grassland renovation. From this small beginning grew Tisbury's biggest industry, manufacturing and exporting farming equipment all over the world. With the closure of the RAF's ammunition depot at Chilmark, the importance of Parmiter's to the local economy became even more starkly emphasized. Sadly, with the shrinking of world markets this, too, was to close in 2004 and awaits future re-development.

above] Gilbert Baker's butcher's shop in 1925. Mr Baker is on the extreme left of the picture.

left] Celebration of the coronation of George V. Among the local celebrities are: Revd F E Hutchinson, J Bristol, E Hibberd and Dr Ensor.

6

West Tisbury
the Vale of Wardour

W HEN DRIVING through the Vale of Wardour, an
area of great beauty, one is conscious of seeing
the English countryside at its most serene.
Here between Tisbury centre and the Donheads there are
stately homes and a ruined castle set among gently rolling
pastureland. It is difficult to imagine this as the scene of
bloody civil war, riots – and an extraordinary ghost story.

The ruins of old Wardour Castle, unusually hexagonal
in shape, are well hidden by the surrounding woodland. The
castle was originally built by Lord John Lovell in 1393 as a
fortified dwelling. In 1547 it was purchased by Sir John
Arundell of Lanherne for his second son, Thomas, as a
wedding present. The bride, Margaret Howard, was the

sister of Catherine, Henry VIII's fourth wife, and it was the grandson of this marriage, another Thomas, who was created the 1st Baron of Wardour by James I. Despite all the political turmoil of the succeeding period and their overt Catholicism, the Arundells have retained the estate almost continuously since then.

It was a daughter of the 1st Lord Arundell who provided Tisbury's second link with the New World. Lady Ann, whose body, like so many of the family's, lies entombed in Tisbury Church, married the 2nd Lord Baltimore. Carrying on the endeavours of his father, Lord Baltimore proceeded with a royal charter to develop an area east of the Potomac River in North America. They sailed on St Cecilia's Day 1633, on a voyage which led to the founding of a new colony, Maryland. Named after Charles I's queen, Henrietta Maria, it became unique for its spirit of religious freedom, a sound Christian belief being all that was required of its citizens.

Ralph Jackson (died 1985) surveying the monumental stone to Lady Ann Arundell in Tisbury church. Ralph was manager of SCATS in Tisbury, but in his spare time studied every aspect of Tisbury history and even taught himself Anglo-Saxon in order to read ancient documents.

Members of the Maryland Militia outside Hook Manor, Donhead St Andrew, to pay tribute to Lady Ann Arundell, 1996

This link with the Arundell family is perpetuated today in the place-names of the state: in Annapolis its capital, in Baltimore its largest city, and in Arundell County. At Hook Manor, Lady Ann's home in the Vale of Wardour, there are plaster mouldings on the ceiling depicting the two ships, the *Ark* and the *Dove,* which took the first settlers on that voyage.

During the Civil War the family strongly supported Charles I and Wardour Castle was besieged on 2 May 1643 by a force of 1,300 parliamentarians. As her husband, the 2nd Lord Arundell, was away fighting for the king, the sixty-year-old Lady Blanche was left with a mere handful of servants and twenty-five fighting men with instructions to protect the castle at all costs. Despite the odds, they held out valiantly for six days until the situation became hopeless. They then surrendered on honourable terms – which were not kept. As her husband died shortly afterwards of wounds sustained at Reading, it was left to their son Henry to recover the castle. This he did after a protracted siege of nearly a year. Eventually, in desperation, he mined his own castle, an action which broke the siege but reduced the castle to a ruin.

As the castle was no longer habitable, the Arundells were forced to live, firstly in a small house south of the bailey wall and then at Breamore in Hampshire. Although returned to favour at the Restoration, the Test Act of 1678 prevented all future members of this staunch Roman Catholic family from holding public office. It was not until the 1760s that their fortunes had revived sufficiently for them to return to Wardour.

The new Wardour Castle, designed for the 8th Lord Arundell by James Paine and completed in 1776, is reputedly the largest Georgian house in Wiltshire. Built of Chilmark stone, it contains within its imposing central section a circular staircase nearly 50 ft in diameter and is flanked on its western side by a quite exceptional chapel, the interior of which was designed by Sir John Soane. Priests had always been associated with Wardour often living rough in the surrounding woodland when religious persecution was at its worst. With the building of the chapel a permanent place of worship was now available. Not before time as, by 1839, 80 per cent of all Roman Catholics in Wiltshire lived on the estate.

right] Bill Targett and friend, itinerants at Wardour in 1907. They travelled around south Wiltshire during the early years of the century carrying out all kinds of jobs in exchange for a hot meal and a night's rest in an outhouse or barn.

Eva Morgan, whose father was a carpenter at Wardour, described her childhood there earlier in the last century:

The community at Wardour was until the end of the Second World War a totally Catholic one, composed of estate workers, tenant farmers and cottagers. It was a very close

left] the magnificent chapel at Wardour Castle

right] The Hon. John Arundell (later 16th and last Lord Arundell) with his sister the Hon Isabel Arundell at the door to the east wing of Wardour Castle in 1928

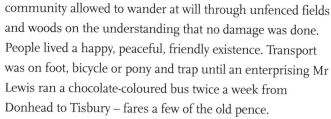

community allowed to wander at will through unfenced fields and woods on the understanding that no damage was done. People lived a happy, peaceful, friendly existence. Transport was on foot, bicycle or pony and trap until an enterprising Mr Lewis ran a chocolate-coloured bus twice a week from Donhead to Tisbury – fares a few of the old pence.

Pleasures were simple and many events took place at the Guildhall. This was a building opened on 18 November 1885. It was erected at the sole expense of old Lady Arundell for the benefit of members of the Guild of St Ignatius and the Guild of the Children of Mary. Here, meetings were held and dances, plays, whist drives, bazaars and other social events. There was a fine stage for dramatic performances and some of the scenery was specially painted by an artist from Paris.

At this time the estate was owned by Lady Anne Arundell, the ageing matriarchal widow of the twelfth lord. Following his death she continued to live at Wardour, presiding over the sale of the estate in 1918 and many of its treasures during a life of increasing eccentricity.

In 1944 the 16th and last Lord Arundell, a much beloved man, died tragically. Having ascended to the title after the death of his father in 1939, he volunteered for the Wiltshire Regiment at the outbreak of war. He was sent to France almost immediately, was wounded near Douai in May 1940 and taken prisoner. After languishing in a number of German prisoner-of-war camps he was transferred to the infamous Colditz fortress after an escape

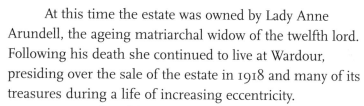

attempt. Here he developed tuberculosis. John Arundell was repatriated to England in September 1944. A great welcome was prepared for him by the family and villagers of Wardour. But it was not to be. Lord John died at Chester soon after his arrival in England. As there was no heir, the title, held for 350 years, finally lapsed.

Nevertheless, the Arundell connection has remained. A great grandson of the ninth baron through the female side took the name of Arundell. Today his son, who inherited the title Lord Talbot of Malahide, continues to live nearby.

Clog makers in the Wardour woods, 1910. The wooden pattens were then transported to the north of England to be finished and sold to the mill workers.

The second notable family to inhabit West Tisbury was the Benetts whose fortunes, if not their religious affiliation, seem to parallel their neighbours at Wardour. Pythouse stands on the opposite side of the Nadder, its prominent facade enjoying a splendid view towards the outer chalk downland of Cranborne Chase. The land was given to the Bennetts (spelt with two 'n's at that time) by the Abbess of Shaftesbury in 1225 and there were probably several manor houses here before the present gracious residence was built.

Like the Arundells, the Bennett family found themselves drawn into the drama of the Civil War although with less enthusiasm. As a result of his support for the Royalist cause and a subsequent heavy fine imposed by parliament, Thomas Bennett became impoverished. Pythouse was sold to the Cromwellian Mayor of Salisbury, Peter Dove, and passed from Bennett hands for fifty-six years.

Matters took a more positive turn for the family when Patience, Thomas's granddaughter, married into a wealthy family at Norton Bavant – strangely, also with the name Bennett but with one 'n'. Their son, another Thomas, later married Etheldred, the daughter of the Archbishop of Canterbury and bought back the property. Here he built a modest, square manor house in Chilmark stone. It was his grandson John who was to add the Palladian extensions built to his own design. These doubled its size and gave Pythouse the classical lines we see today.

John Benett, known as 'Long John' for his slender height, had further enhanced the family fortune by his marriage to Lucy Lambert of Boyton in 1801. As landowner, agrarian reformer and politician he had an enormous influence on the area during the first half of the 19th century. Though obviously able, he was not particularly popular and his campaigns to enter parliament are notable

'Long' John Benett, MP for South Wiltshire and owner of the Pyt House estate. He tried unsuccessfully to prevent the Swing rioters from destroying his threshing machines in 1830.

Pythouse, early 20th century

for the scurrilous and often libellous attacks upon each other by the several candidates and their supporters. 'Benett and Independence', carved deeply into the outside wall of the Boot Inn in Tisbury High Street, was his political slogan. At the hustings he was supported by the Wiltshire Cossacks, in reality a large body of the Hindon troop of Yeoman Cavalry out of uniform who had canvassed on his behalf. Their intimidatory tactics helped to secure his election to parliament in 1819.

Mention has already been made of the dire poverty experienced by rural labourers at the beginning of the 19th century. Thousands of soldiers returning from the Napoleonic Wars flooded the labour market. By 1820, a series of bad harvests, worsened by the Corn Laws keeping up the price of wheat artificially, led to new depths of despair for the working classes.

Sid Dunn in the gate house of the rural crossing at Hatch where his father was in control from 1927 to 1938, then his mother to 1950 before he took over. It was the last crossing on the line to be converted to automatic control, in 1985. At that time Sid, aged 77, was still in charge.

Most bitter to accept, however, was the introduction of mechanisation on farms – especially the hated threshing machines. Set in rich corn-growing land, Tisbury farms provided at least three months' labour for those who could wield a flail. It was backbreaking work but at least it provided a wage. In 1830, as a wave of machine-breaking and rick-burning spread westwards from Kent and Sussex, rural despair in south Wiltshire flared into open rebellion. The Pythouse estate was to suffer the most violent outbreak in the county.

Like many local farmers, John Benett had installed threshing machines on both his farms and knew himself to be a prime target for the aggrieved rioters. Previously warned, he returned in haste from Westminster and arrived at Pythouse at 4 am on 25 November. Four hours later he was woken with news of the mob at Hindon market. He immediately set out to confront them. At Fonthill Gifford he met with some four hundred men armed with axes and sticks. Showing great courage he attempted to reason with them but to no avail. They pressed on to Pythouse Farm destroying other machines on the way.

Their slow progress enabled Benett to arrive before them. It did no good. While he watched from his horse, his threshing machine was broken to pieces. In the melée Benett was hit in the face and knocked unconscious. His other machine at Linley Farm was then attacked before the Hindon Yeoman Cavalry arrived. A pitched battle took place in the woods adjacent to Pythouse. The disorganised mob was no match for this opposition and in the ensuing turmoil one labourer, John Harding, was shot dead.

Twenty-nine prisoners were taken and conveyed to Fisherton Gaol in Salisbury. Fifty years later an aged farm labourer who had witnessed the battle wrote movingly of their terrible journey:

> We had to get our farm horses and wagons and take them to Salisbury – and the blood did trickle out of the wagons the whole way to Salisbury. I was carter and drove the first wagon – when we got to Blackhorse at Chilmark they did cry out for summat to drink, poor fellows, but the cavalry wouldn't let them have nothing. They wouldn't. It were awful cold night and they were most shramm'd with the frost and some on 'em couldn't wag a bit. When we got to Salisbury we took one load to 'firmary and t'others to jail.

As a result of their attack on John Benett's property sixteen men were convicted. Fourteen were transported, mostly to Tasmania, two were sentenced to hard labour and only one acquitted. As Benett was a local senior magistrate and influential in the prosecution as chief witness and foreman of the jury this is not surprising!

One other incident of note during these troubled years concerned Mary Peart, known as Molly, a nursery maid at Pythouse. After becoming pregnant by a father unknown, she murdered her baby and was sentenced to death. She was executed at Oxford around 1824, achieving dubious notoriety as the last woman to be publicly hanged in this country. Her body was originally buried in unhallowed ground but John Benett gained permission for her to be exhumed. The skeleton was articulated, placed in a coffin and returned to Pythouse.

Molly continued to moulder in the wine cellar there for over a century. A tradition grew that by some mysterious means she had threatened to haunt the house if ever she was moved. In 1933 John Benett's great grandson Jack, ignoring such idle speculation, had her moved to a museum at Brighton. At Pythouse, however, noises in the night and family misfortunes are said to have resulted. The coffin, a sombre black casket with a glass viewing window in the front, was hastily returned to the cellars at Pythouse where it remains to this day.

Whatever miseries were suffered by his labourers, John Benett continued to prosper until his death in 1852. His grandson Vere, the new owner of the estate, further consolidated the family wealth by marrying Ellen Stanford, a wealthy lady from Brighton. During his time the property included some 10,000 acres. In 1891 he added the two wings at the back of Pythouse – one with eleven rooms to accommodate visiting cricket teams!

When Vere died in 1894 the family began an era of self-destruction. His widow Ellen, who disliked Pythouse, returned to Brighton where she remarried and left her son John to manage the estate with very little money. John Benett, known as 'Jack', had been a difficult child to handle for both parents. The portrait of mother and son on the top landing of the mansion seems to reflect the lack of affection that existed between them.

John ('Mad Jack') Benett shown in old age with his wife Evelyn

Jack did not inherit Pythouse from his father who thought him too unreliable. Instead he had to rent the estate, by then in a poor condition, from his mother. A bitter legal battle to establish ownership made great inroads into the fortunes of both and it was not until after Ellen's death in the 1930s that his title to the property was confirmed.

As a young man Jack had served in the Boer War and the retreat from Mons during the First World War. He was also a war correspondent and photographer in the Sudan. In later years he became very eccentric and was known locally as 'Mad Jack', a large man with an unpredictable temper. Tales of his strange behaviour still abound in Tisbury. The most common concerns his habit of accosting farm labourers who, during the depression of the Thirties, would often walk miles in their efforts to find a job. He would offer them a lift in his car and order the chauffeur to drive to a

Tisbury unemployed in the 1930s. All were given work by 'Mad Jack' Benett on his Pythouse estate.

remote place. Here he would offer them money and order them to tramp the long journey home.

Jack's only son, Vere, had also served in the First World War and was badly gassed whilst rescuing a sergeant wounded in battle. Although awarded the Military Cross for this act of bravery, he never recovered from the effects of the gas and eventually died in 1922. When Jack himself died in 1947 the Pythouse estate passed from the Benetts forever. His wife, Evelyn, who died ten years later, left it to her cousin Sir Anthony Rumbold, who was living at nearby Hatch House. He sold the property to Mutual Households Association (now Country Houses Association) who preserved the fabric and provided unfurnished apartments for some forty residents until its recent sale to a private owner.

7

Chilmark

Stone of the Finest Quality

THERE IS A RATHER SAD EPITAPH on a weather-worn grave in the local churchyard. It is a mute tribute to numerous generations of quarrymen, most of whom came from Chilmark or Tisbury:

> Here lyeth the body of Phillep Macy who died the 24th day of February in 1711 aged 45 years Hee in his life time engraved stones for many but for himself had no time to engrave any.

Since Norman times, the quarrymen's efforts provided the raw material for some of the finest churches and cathedrals in southern England. Now, the quarry, though largely played out, has blossomed under the tutelage of RAF Chilmark into a conservation area of considerable value. With the withdrawal of this protection by the Ministry of Defence it awaits an uncertain future.

The earliest evidence of quarrying activity at Chilmark is provided by the Romans. Used initially for road-building, the stone was later incorporated into prestigious villas such as those at East Grimstead and Rockbourne. In 1906 a finely-carved Roman bust was excavated at nearby Sutton Mandeville. Coins and jewellery of the period have also been discovered.

With the Norman conquest came the great resurgence of religious building and thus a further impetus for quarrying. The ill-fated cathedral at Old Sarum was built with Chilmark stone. Two centuries later, from Chilmark and Tisbury came stone for the new cathedral more conveniently situated in the new city of Salisbury in the

A team of workers cutting stone from the face at Chilmark quarry, early 20th century

valley below. When the elegant spire was added in the 14th century it was again Chilmark that provided the 6,000 tons of material required.

By the 17th century most farmhouses, cottages and barns in south Wiltshire, as well as the magnificent manors of the wool merchants, were built from this source. The difficulties of transport, however, made it too costly for wider use. In the late 18th century two canals and, later, the railway were constructed in the north of Wiltshire. This gave a great advantage to the quarry owners of the Box and Corsham area who could market their product far more cheaply than those in the south. However, when the Salisbury to Yeovil railway was developed in 1859, it brought the track alongside the River Nadder passing only a mile to the south of the quarry with stations at Dinton and Tisbury. Thus, the situation changed and Chilmark stone became cheaper and more extensively available. Its subsequent use included the large circular window in the north transept of Westminster Abbey, the restoration of Chichester and Rochester cathedrals and the abbeys at St Albans and Romsey.

Although Chilmark owes its existence from Roman times to the stone quarries, agriculture has always been its main preoccupation. To the north lies chalk downland, an area of sheep pasture and large arable fields, in contrast to the south of the village where the quarries lie. Here the fields remain smaller and there is much more woodland. To the west is the remote hamlet of Ridge where the parish abuts Fonthill Park. Here you can enjoy the beautiful vistas of Lady Down where older open-cast quarries lie long discarded.

Between these extremes is the picturesque village centre where the cottages of Becketts Lane and The Street meet at a point called The Cross. Many are of the 17th century and were previously covered with a rougher type of thatch drooping down over the windows and looking, as one local farmer put it, 'like a very shaggy bobtailed old English sheepdog with its eyes peeping out'. They show the local Portland stone at its best for domestic architecture, the cream-coloured sandy limestone, now weathered grey and overspread with lichen. A winter bourn, crossed by miniature bridges, flanks The Street and gathers pace as it joins the Nadder further south.

The name of Chilmark had been recorded in various forms during the Saxon and Norman periods but Stone and Bronze Age remains indicate primitive settlements long before the Romans came. The Domesday Book of 1086 confirms that Chilmark was part of the estate of the Abbess of Wilton, passing at the Dissolution through the Herbert family to the Earls of Pembroke.

The churchyard is entered through a lych-gate, a memorial to Emma Lindsell who was killed when thrown from her pony and trap. The church itself is dedicated to St Margaret of Antioch possibly by returning Crusaders and stands imposingly at the top of a steep lane known as Barberry. Parts of the church go back to the 13th century – the lancet windows, the 'priest's' doorway in the chancel and the outside corbels – but an earlier church on the

left] Becketts Lane, Chilmark, in 1910 looking towards the church

site would have pre-dated this by many centuries. The porch, where in earlier times religious ceremonies and civil business were conducted, was added in the 14th century. The handsome spire came much later in 1770.

The Black Dog, an early 18th-century hostelry, once one of three in the village, stands on the ancient road which later took the stage-coach traffic through to its staging post at Hindon. In the field opposite, a sheep fair was held annually on 20 July, St Margaret's Day.

The diminutive Chilmark Manor is of the early 17th century but has been much altered since. It lies below the church on the corner of the Cross. Entered through a surprisingly small courtyard, it is fronted by a scrolled wall. Diana Forbes, whose parents bought nearby Chilmark House in 1930, loved to visit the two old ladies who lived in

Harry Jukes outside the Black Dog, Chilmark, in the early 1930s. He was the landlord there 1892 to 1942.

the manor: 'They kept pigeons which they called "The Nuns" after the nuns who had lived in the Manor when it was an offshoot of the Wilton Convent. They had a cricket in the wall above their fireplace and we used to hear it singing in the evening when we went to tea with them.'

Further east along The Street lies the Old Rectory, probably Chilmark's oldest building. Its age is uncertain but a document of 1588 mentions 'a house wherein a curate did commonly live'. An intriguing late-Victorian ghost story associated with this house was found with the deeds in 1936 when Mr Hardwick purchased the property.

During the 1890s, the Rev. G Herbert Johnson, Diocesan Missioner to Bishop Wordsworth, visited the rectory. He was there to support a curate in residence during the absence of the vicar, Charles March Tower, who was wintering with his family abroad. Whilst he was there he saw the apparition of a girl appearing and disappearing in the passageway. The housekeeper, who presumably saw it too, became frightened but was dissuaded from her wish to leave. The curate's wife, however, departed after seeing the curtains to the four-poster bed move and someone leaning over her sighing and moaning. The experience made her so ill a nurse had to be summoned.

Whether or not these events were the result of hysteria, some time later the skeleton of a girl was discovered under a west facing window during drainage repairs. The builders also discovered a hollow section of wall in the hall which they wished to open. A written request was sent to the Rev. Charles Tower but permission was refused. It appears that Mr Tower had been guardian to a girl many years previously and made it known that his ward had gone to visit distant relations in the colonies. Was there, literally, a skeleton in the vicar's cupboard? We shall never know.

Mary Evans died in 1992 at the age of ninety-six. She retained remarkably clear memories of Chilmark at the turn of the last century and of her grandmother, a grand dame of the local community:

In my childhood, Chilmark was a charming, quite unspoiled village: hardly any traffic, and that only horse-drawn, with its small stone cottages, thickly thatched, with the typical Wiltshire shallow chalk-stream of clear water in front of them; bright green in patches with water-cress, and great flag-stones laid as bridges across for each cottage. . . . The hedges were rampant with honeysuckle, wild roses, traveller's joy, wild flowers, blackberry and hazel nuts.

Grannie was an ardent Protestant and gave us books to read on Sunday like *Almost a Nun*. She was very good and of the highest principles, but she often fell out with her clergymen! At one time, perhaps when her vicar was rather high church, she gave/built/paid for a chapel for Chilmark, being herself very low church. Perdita (my daughter) has the silver dish of pretty openwork with an engraved inscription that was given to her, in thanks, by the congregation.

There is a story from that chapel: one of its members, Bill Sprackland, had a father who, being an elder

Old farmhouse, now Vine Cottage at the Cross, Chilmark, before 1900. In front is a fine example of a Wiltshire boat wagon, probably made by wheelwright Francis Harding, who is holding the horse.

of another chapel, was asked one day when visiting his son to lead the congregation in prayer. His prayer was 'Gard bless Oi, (pause) moi woif (pause). Moi zun Bill, (pause) 'is woif (a longer pause) Uz vower, no mower, A—men.'

My grandmother was a very strong character. She used to lecture carters and draymen about careless unkindness to their horses: like the abominable bearing rein which held the horse's head so high that he lost much of his power to pull; like uncomfortable bits and thoughtless beatings. She was a wonderful grandmother bringing her strong, Christian principles into our daily life.

The grandmother in question was Mary Whitehead, a member of the wealthy King family of Chilmark House. One of her daughters, Lucy Flower, died aged 104 in 1967. The Flower family had been farming locally for many years and her husband James, with his Hampshire Down sheep, became one of the finest sheep breeders of his day winning more than seven hundred prizes at the leading agricultural shows.

But the Kings were influential landowners and the Flowers tenant farmers. To view the lives of ordinary villagers we must turn to the diaries of Edwin Rixon, a stonemason and son of James Rixon mentioned previously, who carved the stone heads still seen in odd corners of Tisbury.

As a general rule, diaries which survive the deaths of their owners are the creation of the more leisured classes. Alternatively, they may be the product of busy professionals whose lives are somehow tied up with events of national or cultural significance. Rixon, however, was an artisan who spent much of his working life in the Chilmark Quarries and later helped to maintain the roads of southern Wiltshire. The value of these documents, written between 1904 and his death in 1952 at the age of eighty-six, lies in the view they give us of rural domestic existence during the first half of the last century.

Edwin Rixon lived with his wife Emma and children, Doris, Fred and Isobel, in at least two different rented cottages at Chilmark during the first period of the 19th century. They were annually affected by flooding, problems of sanitation and inadequate well-water, as well as the incursions of rats. Edwin often walked long distances to Tisbury or to his

Chilmark

Chilmark Brass Band, early 20th century. Edwin Rixon, whose diaries assisted with the research for this book, is seated third from the left.

places of work because the valley roads were impassable by bicycle, which was his usual mode of transport.

Edwin was associated with the Chilmark, Tisbury and Fovant Brass Bands, following a tradition which spread back through his family and forward into the future. (His grandson Robert Hardy was for many years conductor of the Wilton British Legion Band). Rixon often travelled with his family to Victoria Park in Salisbury or the Salvation Army Citadel to hear concerts. Music was the first pleasure he noted when obtaining a wireless in 1926. His brother's zither and a friend's harmonium were two of the many instruments brought to him for repair.

In 1907 Mr T T Gething took out a lease on the Chilmark Quarry where Edwin Rixon was already working. Gething had previously owned a stone business at Kensington and was the London agent for Chilmark stone so he was obviously well known in the area. Rixon's position must have been one of some responsibility as he was timekeeper and in charge of the smooth running of the machinery, an occupation which caused him much heartache. There are constant references to leaking boilers and the difficulties of maintaining steam, belts slipping off flywheels and faulty drills which necessitated trips to Ingersolls in London. There were accidents particularly on the saw frames and damage to the crane used for lifting the massive slabs of stone.

Mr T T Gething and son with workers at Chilmark quarry, early 20th century. Mr Gething is on the extreme left and his son extreme right. Mr Gething leased the quarry from 1907 until it was taken over by the Ministry of Defence in the mid-1930s. It was partly re-opened in 1981 to provide stone for Salisbury Cathedral.

Even before the First World War, the spread of mechanised traffic was beginning to affect the self-sufficiency of village life. At Chilmark, Ted Street provided the village carrier service to Salisbury twice a week, bringing back, in the words of Maurice Flower, 'anything from a reel of cotton or bloomer elastic to a pig from market for the cottagers' sties'. This was to be supplemented by the remarkable enterprise of two brothers.

After leaving school at fourteen, Fred Viney worked at the quarry at that time part-owned by his uncle, Levi Bowles. Early one frosty September morning, Fred, by this time a sixteen-year-old, was crushed under a rock fall. He was taken to Salisbury Infirmary in a passing wagon where his entire right leg had to be removed. Reg Viney, his brother, had lost his left arm following an accident as a child.

In 1917 Tom Viney, another uncle who owned a smallholding in the village, offered to give the brothers some capital if they could make a go of it. Remarkably, they chose to buy a bus. Can you imagine that: a one-armed conductor and a one-legged driver! The Viney's first bus was called *The Victory*. Fred drove it with his single leg and his one-armed brother operated the ticket machine with great dexterity. Both men worked long hours to build up a

The Viney's bus ran from Chilmark to Salisbury from 1917. Fred, the one-legged driver, is on the right. Reg, the one-armed conductor, is seated at the front of the bus.

The Vineys' first bus, 'The Victory', posed in Salisbury. Reg, the conductor, stands in front, while Fred is seated behind the wheel.

successful and hugely popular service operating from Chilmark to Salisbury. A later bus was larger, a thirty-two-seater, and on one occasion 92 people were counted dismounting at the Salisbury terminus in New Canal!

Up and down the valley I have heard nothing but praise for the Viney bus. Charlie Merrifield, for example, a farm labourer's son living at Teffont from the early thirties, remembers Christmas Eve:

> We nearly always went to Salisbury. This would be after tea as Dad and the other men would have to work until 5 o'clock. This was on Fred and Reg Viney's bus, of course. We stayed in Salisbury as late as the bus would allow so as to see what we could pick up cheap. Meat, poultry and fruit were always sold off at the end of the day as there was little then in the way of keeping it.
>
> There was an approximate time for the bus to leave. This was to say the least very, very flexible. The Vineys knew

every person that they had taken into Salisbury with them and would not leave until all were on board for the return journey. If for some reason some people were not coming home they would say so. I have known Reg Viney go around the pubs near to the Canal to find his passengers. When he brought them back a big cheer would be given. I can never remember any cross words over a person that was late in returning.

When the bus did eventually leave (it was I believe a twenty-eight seater Albion at that time) it was quite literally packed to the roof. There were more standing than were sat. All that were seated had a child on their lap.

Not only did the brothers take passengers but they also received orders for goods in Salisbury. Fred would deliver the items up and down the valley with the produce – which included groceries, fish and chips and cases of bloaters – tucked under his single arm.

The Viney's successful business continued throughout the twenties and thirties with two additional buses being purchased. After Reg's death in 1940, Fred remained actively involved in the valley transport until his death thirty-four years later.

Messrs T T Gething and sons were still the owners of the quarry in 1930. By that time they must have updated their equipment considerably for they were able to claim 'an amplitude of good stone, the most up-to-date machinery and a sufficiency of skilled labour'. By 1935 the effects of the Depression led builders to look elsewhere for cheaper building materials. The quarry closed although partly re-opened in 1981 to provide enough stone for the restoration of Salisbury Cathedral spire.

From the mid-thirties, the quarry area served as a supply depot for the RAF, surely one of the most attractive in the country. The base continually made efforts to blend with the area, maintaining close links with the Nature Conservancy Council (now Natural England). It is a boon to geologists, botanists and biologists alike who visit the area frequently. This is hardly surprising. There are ten species of bat in the caves; no other hibernation centre in the British Isles has so many.

Thanks to the dedication of staff and local residents under expert leadership, many other forms of monitoring take place at RAF Chilmark where the flora, including eight

A large block of stone being winched on to a trolley at Chilmark quarry, early 20th century

different species of orchid, is rich and varied. The summer and winter passage of migrant birds continues to be monitored, as well as a butterfly and moth survey which has identified six hundred different varieties. Within the grounds are two types of protected newts. Fungi identification takes place with the help of Salisbury Natural History Society.

Unless a satisfactory alternative is found, the government decision to close RAF Chilmark could have devastating social and economic effects on the Nadder Valley community. In addition, future generations of nature lovers – who have seen in Chilmark a haven for so many threatened species of our environment – will view its closure with great regret.

8

The Teffonts
Magna and Evias

EDITH OLIVIER, the diarist and daughter of a Wilton
rector, dreamed of living at Fitz House, Teffont
Magna. She accomplished this in the early 1920s. It
was a handsome residence, she wrote, built by 17th-century
wool merchants, where water bubbled up under every room
and kept the grass of the beautiful gardens perpetually
green.

> When as children we sometimes drove to parties at Fonthill,
> we always passed a most romantic house which I used to
> long to have for my own. This was Fitz House in Teffont,
> which many people call the prettiest of all Wiltshire villages.
> Just beyond the end of its street, a tiny stream gushes out of

Teffont Magna main street in about 1900, with the old school (beyond the bicycle) and St Edward's church in the background

the chalk down, to flow the whole length of the village in front of the houses, each of which has its own little bridge connecting it with the highway. This water is said to be the purest in Wiltshire: it is very clear, and it tinkles with a silver voice. Fitz House had lately been bought by our friend Lord Bledisloe and he now offered to let it to us. So this house of my childish dreams became the first in which Mildred and I were raised to the dignity of being householders.

The Teffont villages, Magna and Evias, are linked by the crystal water of the River Teff which rises at Springhead. Here, at the foot of the down, a blue bead was found at the throat of a skeleton interred with little dignity in prehistoric times. The tiny river follows the course of the busy B3089 to the Black Horse Inn (now a publishing house) where it continues its journey to Teffont Evias and the grounds of its manor house and church. Here, its waters are dammed by an artificial lake, beloved of swans and herons, before joining its confluence with the Nadder further south by the mill.

It is difficult to imagine that a diminutive country lane running north of Teffont Magna from the church to Dinton was once the main coaching road but you can still see the old toll house and the original Black Horse Inn in close proximity. With the creation of a new turnpike road through the village in the early 19th century the inn licence passed to the new Black Horse, which was previously an 18th-century farmhouse.

Historically, Teffont Magna's fortunes were linked with neighbouring Dinton. Throughout the Middle Ages they remained jointly a manor of Shaftesbury Abbey, passing after the Dissolution to the Pembroke family at Wilton. In 1919 Teffont Magna was sold to Lord Bledisloe

The Wilton Hunt outside the Black Horse Inn at Teffont in the mid-1930s. Lucy Lee, daughter of Robert Lee, the Teffont Manor coachman/ chauffeur, is on the right selling poppies for Armistice Day.

who is still remembered as a benevolent landowner. Until
1922 the church, too, was a mere chapel-of-ease to Dinton
and no land was consecrated for burial purposes until 1925.
Until then the dead of Teffont Magna were carried
arduously along the 'Coffin Path' that weaves its way across
the common to Dinton Church over a mile to the east.

St Edward's Church at Teffont Magna is named after
its association with Shaftesbury Abbey and nestles behind
the village school which closed in 1936. It is much older

left] The last pupils to attend
Teffont Church Junior School
in 1936. Pupils then
transferred to the new Wilton
Secondary School and Dinton
Primary. With them is the vicar,
Revd Keatinge Clay.

right] A combine harvester,
reputedly the first to be used
in England, at Manor Farm,
Teffont Magna, 1934. It came
from the International
Harvester Company of
America. Jim Brockway is the
tractor driver, and Bill Crouch,
the farmer, is at the controls.
Charlie Merrifield is one of
two boys hidden at the back.
The other is John Read, the
farmer's nephew.

than the manorial church at Teffont Evias, its simplicity
reflecting its humbler origin. Believed to be late 13th
century, it was built on the site of an earlier church of which
the two fragments of a Saxon Cross near the entrance may
have been a part. Scratched on the door jambs of the south
porch are two medieval ships, unusual for an inland church.

Through this entrance passed little Mary Humby. She was the tenth child of her parents and when she was taken to her baptism had a sprig of myrtle attached so that she could not be claimed by the curate as a tithe! In the nave of the church can be seen a narrow-waisted bell – one of the few to have survived in England.

Behind the church, Teffont Magna continues along a downland road to Farmer Giles, a farm geared today as much to leisure pursuits as to the needs of the agricultural market.

Charlie Merrifield came to the village in 1930 at the age of seven when the Fisher Crouch family moved from Dorset to take on Manor Farm. His father, a farm labourer,

moved with them and, with a net weekly income of twenty-three shillings and sevenpence, the family, like so many others, found life difficult. At that time, however, it was a busy community with 124 people employed within the two Teffont villages. Of these, twenty-eight worked on Manor Farm alone. Charlie's diary of the thirties, preserved for his daughter, shows the Nadder Valley to have been remarkably self-sufficient despite the ravages of the Depression:

> A shop on the corner was kept by Harry Ells. There was another midway down the village known as Cox's shop. Mr Cox also had a small holding and delivered milk from a covered bucket or two hung on a pedal cycle and measured into your jugs at the door. He also killed his own pigs, sold pork and offal locally and cured his own bacon.

above] Pea pickers at Teffont in the 1930s. At four old pence per basket it was hard work!

left] Visiting the smithy, a pastoral scene at Teffont Evias, early 20th century. Ralph Stevens is leading horses to be shoed at Harry Bull's forge, which stood beside the road leading between the two Teffont villages.

The general store of William Thomas Brooks at Teffont Evias in 1905, which stands (now a private house) opposite the former Black Horse. Mr Brooks was formerly a shoemaker at Dinton and his wife Catherine Jane ran the post office at Teffont.

The Black Horse Inn was a fully licensed pub run by Mr and Mrs Mann. The Post Office was just below the Black Horse in the house now called the Old Forge. Next door was Harry Bull's blacksmith's shop. The village undertaker, carpenter and jobbing builder was Sidney Street who also ran a small holding. The stone quarry was still being worked then but the lime kiln ceased working just prior to our arrival.

By this time, mechanisation had enabled traders to extend their businesses throughout the valley. Three bakers delivered daily to the village. In addition they all delivered groceries and fruit as well as hen and pig food. There were also three butchers. A van belonging to Fred James of Fovant – described by Charlie as 'the forerunner of the mobile shop'- called twice a week with groceries, paraffin oil and methylated spirits.

Among the more colourful characters to ply their wares in the Teffonts at this time were Ossie Coward who came every two months with an open lorry piled high with second-hand furniture and Cyril Hart who drove his motorcycle from Sherrington to pick up boots and shoes for repair. Sweepy Mullins also arrived with a motorcycle fitted with a sidecar. Henry Buckle travelled on a pedal cycle from Salisbury with a large container on the front, the door of which let down as a serving hatch. It was of such a size that he could only just look over the top when cycling. He sold garden seeds of very good quality, then slyly produced religious tracts from the pocket of his long, dark coat. The earnestness of his approach was such that his profit from these was often more than from the seeds!

Opposite the Black Horse, a minor road sweeps into the village of Teffont Evias. It is a most pleasing experience to follow the roadside stream past the manor house and church to the junction with the winding Dinton to Tisbury road. The view here has been aptly described as one of the finest in the county. The name Evias (or Ewyas) is derived from the Manor of Ewyas Harold in Herefordshire's Golden Valley. The family of Ewyas who lived there also owned land in Teffont until the 13th century.

The church of St Michael and All Angels stands in the manor grounds, its beautiful 125 ft steeple seeming to spring directly from the soil. The north chapel is mid-15th century and contains the tombs of Henry Ley and two of his sons, their dusty effigies shown in medieval armour. A younger son, James, who subsequently became the first Earl of Marlborough and Lord Chief Justice of England, was made rector of the church at the age of eighteen. His duties could not have proved arduous; while the salary enabled him to study in London, the butler took the services on his behalf!

The north chapel is the oldest part of the building. Except for parts of the chancel and nave walls, it is all that is left of the medieval church rebuilt by the Lord of the Manor, John Mayne, in 1821. Particularly interesting are the windows of the nave containing roundels of small Flemish pictures. They are Biblical scenes probably the work of 17th-century artists. The beautifully-illustrated Teffont WI Scrapbook of 1956, rather inaccessibly kept under glass, is also of note. Compiled for a national competition, it is a fine tribute to the

Teffont Evias Manor House, c.
1900

painstaking efforts of WI members all over the country,
whose investigations preserved much of local interest that
would otherwise have disappeared.

The manor house, with its outbuildings and cottages,
seems to run into the wooded hillside. Although of late
Tudor origin, much that we see today was added by John
Mayne in the early 19th century including the battlemented
porch and the tall circular tower. The water tower to the
north-west was added later in the century. It was from here
that fireworks used to be lit during lavish Boxing Day
parties given to the villagers. Teffont Evias had been in the
possession of the Mayne family since 1679 and the manor
remains the property of their descendants. However, it has
been leased to a variety of families since they gave up
residence during the late 19th century.

Robert Lee came to the manor as coachman and later
chauffeur in 1897. His employer until 1920 was Charles

left] Photograph published in the Motor Magazine of May 1908 showing Charles Maudslay with his chauffeur Robert Lee. Robert had come to Teffont Manor as coachman, but Maudslay had 'sent him to Coventry' to learn to drive when he changed over from coach to car.

Maudslay, one member of the family celebrated for its achievements in the fields of engineering and vehicle manufacture. The Maudslay Marine Engine, for example, enabled *The Great Western,* one of the first steamships, to cross the Atlantic from Bristol to New York in 1837. Charles Maudslay and 'Mad Jack' Benett of Pythouse were the first in the valley to own their own cars.

right] The Tennant family at Teffont Manor (which they had leased) with famous theatrical friends in 1935. Left to right: Angela Baddeley, Hermione Tennant (the actress Hermione Baddeley), Rosemary Mark-Kerr, Jill Esmond (first wife of Laurence Olivier), David Tennant, Laurence Olivier. The Tennants were at Teffont Manor until the war.

left] Robert Lee, chauffeur at the manor, brought up his family here at Teffont Manor Lodge. The house survives at the junction of the B3089 and the Tisbury turning, which in the early 20th century was still gated.

Robert Lee lived in the tiny lodge at the junction of the B3089 and the Tisbury road, a point that was gated until the necessities of war led to their removal in the 1940s. In this small lodge Robert and his wife Emma brought up their family of six children and continued to serve a succession of the manor house tenants. Probably the most flamboyant of these were the Hon. David Tennant and his wife, the actress Hermione Baddeley. A photograph in the *Tatler* of November 1935 shows a house party which included the actor Laurence Olivier with his first wife, Jill Esmond. These occasions could be quite wild. Guests are remembered leaping across the large garden pond – not always successfully – and even jumping a bonfire on one occasion.

During the Second World War, the manor was used extensively by the army. Important maps of the Normandy Landings were printed on mobile presses in the parkland. After the war Sir Edgar Keatinge decided to convert the property into three flats.

The quarry mentioned by Charlie Merrifield lies on Butts Hill in a woody area to the west of the church. The stone face is now hidden beneath dense vegetation but the remains of Roman artefacts indicate its early use. It should not be confused with its more famous

neighbour at Chilmark, part of which is known as Teffont
Quarry and would have provided much of the stone for
village cottages. The Butts Hill quarry, still providing some
stone in 1947, was linked by rail to the two lime kilns in
Carters Lane. Donkey-driven trucks full of waste stone
would be hauled to the kilns along this track and fired to
provide lime for mortar and agricultural use.

In 1922 the two Teffont villages were joined into one
parish and the lively community described by Charlie
Merrifield continued until shortly after the Second World
War. Today at Manor Farm, the largest of the Teffont farms,
only two labourers are required to tend the 1,000 acres
previously tilled by twenty-eight. Not surprisingly, many old
cottages have disappeared from the village or have merged
to provide higher-class accommodation.

Attempts to diversify into the leisure industry – like
the promising shire-horse centre and a partly constructed
golf course that laid waste to the common – have come to
naught. Perhaps the Farmer Giles Educational Unit, now
developed into an entertainment centre, will be more
fortunate.

9

Dinton

Sheep, Orchards and Water Meadows

THERE IS A STRANGE VERSE, recorded on a small brass plate near the altar of St Mary the Virgin Church, Dinton, in memory of Roger Earth who died in 1634:

> From Earth we came to Earth wee must return
> Witnes this Earth that lyes within this urn
> Begott by Earth borne also on Earth's wombe
> 74 Yeares liv'd Earth now Earth his tombe
> In Earth Earth's body lyes under this stone
> But from this Earth to heaven Earth's soule is gone

It marks the end of an era, for the Earths were the last family to farm Dinton with Teffont Magna as one estate. Henceforth the two villages could develop their separate identities more easily despite the continuing ecclesiastical ties.

St Mary's was another of the Nadder Valley churches to rise, phoenix-like, from the ruins of an earlier Saxon one. Throughout the Middle Ages, its sturdy tower marked the eastern edge of the estates of Shaftesbury's Benedictine Abbey. Its nave, crossing and transepts all date from the 12th century. Later additions and restorations – the last by William Butterfield, a noted Victorian architect – have moulded well to create a very handsome building well cherished through the centuries by wealthy benefactors.

To the south and east lay the estates of that other great abbey at Wilton. With the Dissolution of the Monasteries the power of both was broken. The Manor of Dinton passed, first to Sir Thomas Arundell in 1540 and, after his execution for felony, to Sir William Herbert, the 1st Earl of Pembroke. Laurence Hyde lived at Hatch House near Tisbury. He purchased from the Pembrokes the patronage of Dinton Church and the rectory. Here his grandson Edward was born – the future 1st Lord of Clarendon and Chancellor to Charles II.

left] Dinton Fête Day, about 1904. The Wyndham Arms Slate Club band and officials lead the procession from the church after their service.

Through her secret marriage to the Duke of York (later James II), Edward's daughter Mary gave birth to two future monarchs of England, Mary and Anne. Although the rectory has long since disappeared, it was replaced in the 18th century by the elegant Wren-style building we see today. Now owned by the National Trust, it is known as Hyde House in memory of the family.

Snowhill, an unspoilt back lane opposite the church, passes the old stone farmhouses of Cotterell and Jesse, names found in the earliest of parish records. The last residence in Snowhill, before it merges with the busy B3089, is Lawes Cottage, believed to have been the home of Henry Lawes, a contemporary of Edward Hyde. He became Master of the King's Musick and one of the outstanding musicians of his day

By the late 17th century, the ancient Wyndham family had purchased land in Dinton and Sutton Mandeville. Their

'Miss Penn' – Miss Constance Penruddocke, sister of Charles Penruddocke of Compton Park. She lived at Cotterells, Dinton, and was much respected for her hospitality to 1st World War troops, especially Australians.

estate, passing from father to eldest son, increased
sufficiently throughout the 18th and early 19th centuries to
rival that of their powerful Nadder Valley neighbours, the
Pembrokes and the Arundells. It centred on Dinton Park
where in 1816 they developed an earlier residence into the
present-day neo-classical mansion with its imposing Ionic
portico. It was created by Jeffrey Wyatt (or Wyattville) who is
believed to have based his design on John Benett's Pythouse
near Tisbury. In 1917, William Wyndham sold his Dinton
property to Bertram Erasmus Philipps.

Gladys Gipson, was for many years the village
postmistress and recalled her isolation while growing up on
the estate:

> The thatched house where I lived was right off the beaten
> track. Our nearest neighbours were at least two fields away.
> We had no water in the house and the nearest well was 500
> yards away. My father, Vivian Townsend, who was
> gamekeeper to Mr Philipps, always had working dogs and,
> therefore, we were not allowed to have pets. He kept a good
> garden as well as bees – the fields were not sprayed in those
> days so there was plenty of honey. Mother kept chickens
> and wild rabbits were plentiful too. It was not until we
> began to walk the 1½ miles to school that we knew anything
> about the village at all.

The Philippses, too, must have found life lonely as
they left Dinton House for the former rectory, Hyde House,
nearer the village centre. In 1940 they leased their former

left] Mr Darling, of the Wyndham estate in 1900.He came from Scotland in 1840 as bailiff and steward of Dinton House, and caused much mirth at first as he wore a kilt – not seen before by local villagers. He is shown in front of his home at Marshwood.

below left] Vivian Townsend, gamekeeper to Bertram Erasmus Philipps of Dinton House, 1916-40 (now known as Philipps house). With him are his wife and Gladys, one of his two daughters.

right] Students of the itinerant dairy school run by Wiltshire County Council, learning the techniques of cheesemaking at Fitz Farm, Dinton, in 1912.

home to the YMCA and in 1945 gave the house with its surrounding parkland to the National Trust. From that time on it was known as Philipps House. It is remarkable that a village as small as Dinton has seven National Trust properties, of which Philipps House, Hyde House, Lawes Cottage and Little Clarendon – once famous for its owner's cultivation of daffodils – are the most notable.

To the north, the village is bounded by Grim's Ditch, fringing the forest of Grovely. Here, from a height of 600 ft, it drops southwards to the Nadder. Its landscape, once grazed by multitudes of sheep, is bisected by the Roman road which led from Old Sarum to the Mendip lead mines. It is also scarred by the ancient track of the Ox Drove where, until the 1850s, the New Inn provided refreshment for passing travellers. This downward progression to the valley is arrested by a windswept ridge – much quarried for sand – which carried the old toll road to Teffont. Below, just north

of Philipps House, is the isolated mound of Wick Ball Camp, an Iron Age fortress.

Between this ridge and the Nadder lies the village centre. Originally clustered around the church, its age-old economy of corn and sheep was dramatically enhanced from the 17th century with the new practice of 'flooding' or 'drowning' the meadows. The initial investment in hatches, sluices and ditches to distribute the water evenly over the low-lying fields was high but the results in earlier grazing for the flocks and bigger hay crops well repaid this outlay. It must have caused quite a flurry in the village as the flocks moved in springtime from the arable downland to graze on the new grass.

Walter Lake came to Dinton in the 1880s when sheep were still driven in vast numbers along the ancient green ways to Wilton Fair. Gamekeeper to Squire Wyndham, he was a massive man but so light on his feet he could jump a five bar gate with his gun in his hand! Gordon Lake, his grandson, still remembered the value of the water meadows and regretted their passing:

> In this valley sizeable systems started, I believe, at Tisbury and numbered at least ten before the Nadder River is lost to the Avon River. The basic principle was to irrigate as large an area of grassland as possible with the warm river water, thus promoting growth.
>
> The Dinton system covered about 130 acres; its main hatches are a little upstream from the Dinton/Fovant road and are today still a substantial structure. It was known to hundreds of youngsters as 'Twelvehatch'll', though labelled 'Daniel's Hatches' on the Dinton Award Map.

Dinton

When artificial manures came, water meadows were no longer necessary and from the late 1930s they declined. It was always difficult to get the farm wagons around the channels, I know, but the grass had a most glorious smell especially when it was cut to make hay!

Between the ridge and the meadows, the village rests on a strip of greensand. This proved eminently suitable for the orchards and market gardening which formed a further plank in the village economy. An 18th-century observer remarked that when the fruit trees were in bloom, a traveller might suppose he was in Devon or Herefordshire.

With the creation of the railway in 1859, Dinton provided the only station between Wilton and Tisbury. This brought fresh prosperity to the village, as not only was its local market considerably enlarged, but farmers from neighbouring parishes arrived to complete their journey to Salisbury Market by train. The original Wyndham Arms,

Dinton Station, c. 1915. Assembled on the platform are George Glidden, porter, James Vanstone, porter and booking clerk (parish clerk and churchwarden, 1890), Mr Lillington, stationmaster, Stanley Lillington, booking clerk, and John Jones, signalman 1889-1926. On the line is Frank Dowdell, plate-layer, who was still working in 1956.

next to the station, had to extend its stabling to accommodate the increasing trade. The WI Scrapbook of 1956 records the gritty, comradely nature of Dinton's 'golden age'. Perhaps the comparative prosperity of the local economy explains the peace that reigned in Dinton during the 1830 riots when Tisbury, Wilton and Barford St Martin suffered so badly.

above right] William Wyatt (1871-1938), Grandmaster of Oddfellows Lodge, Dinton, early last century. A practised thatcher and Dinton's sub-postmaster for 33 years. He was also church organist at Compton Chamberlayne, where he was born, and later at Baverstock, where he conducted the Dinton Choral Society and hand-bell ringers, and was captain of the church bell-ringers.

Emmanuel Penny is recorded as seeing the first train pass through the village with its open-truck carriages carrying the railway directors all wearing top hats. Mary Ann Burton (née Hibberd) first made the journey by train to Tisbury as a baby. Her mother carried her along roads from Chicksgrove so thick with mud that she wore wooden pattens and changed into her shoes at Dinton station.

Cecil Clark remembered the cutting of 10 acres of wheat in 1899. Two men started work before dawn with scythes and sickles. At breakfast time their wives and children arrived with food for the day, remaining to tie up the sheaves. They completed 1½ to 2 acres a day with each

family receiving 6s for a day's work. This Herculean task might well have been matched by other farm workers. William Barnes, a roadman, John Musselwhite and a labourer called Charlton were expert mowers who were employed during the hay harvest by Dinton farmers at so much an acre. They worked almost continuously from daybreak to dusk, each man quenching his thirst with around 3 gallons of cider a day.

The village was always well serviced. Although the post office has been located at several different points, the village shop has remained in its central position at the end of Snowhill for over a century. Rebuilt by Lord Pembroke in 1902 from old farm cottages, it brought together shop, bakery and dwelling house. Today it also embraces the post office thus providing a commercial centre that many villages might envy. A wheelwright, Walter Clark, produced wagons of a very high quality and the Baker family with their forge

right] Reg Baker, the Dinton blacksmith, early 20th century. His forge on the corner of Spracklands has been replaced by modern houses.

on the corner of Spracklands, served the village as blacksmiths for generations.

In 1904 Dinton Brickyard, situated in Brack Lane, was opened by the Pembroke Estate. This included a pottery works as well as three large brick kilns. Thus, on one site, the production of drain pipes, tiles and garden ornaments was carried on alongside the manufacture of bricks to fuel the ever increasing requirements of the local builders.

Lou Winters's book, *Tales of a Carter's Daughter,* gives a clear picture of Dinton in the early part of the last century. Born in 1898, she arrived in the village at the age of seven. Her father was the carter at Jesses Farm in charge of a team of six horses. She worked as a maid of all sorts in the farmhouse. It was a terror to clean, with its cast-iron range, scullery and washroom complete with iron pump and copper. For 4*d* an hour, (rising to 8*d*) she even had to take home washing to be done. When her father developed epilepsy thirty years later, he could no longer work with animals or machinery and was immediately sacked.

left] Dinton brick works employees, c. 1927

Lou Winters's book reminds us that, even in Dinton, deprivation existed:

> People were really poor, farm wages being eight shillings and ten shillings per week for a seven-day week. No days off, no holidays. Milking and care of animals and horses had to be done even on Sundays. I've heard many an old lady say she could never go out as she had no clothes to wear.
>
> Children wore the clothes which had been handed down by some better-off folk. Mother would unpick and wash any garment and remake things for her family. Hobnail boots were all the family had, one pair each, and on Saturday night they had to be cleaned in readiness for Sunday. Little boys wore big flat white collars or a sailor's collar over their jackets. Mothers would do their best to make little girls look as nice as they could, even if only with a pretty frilly pinafore. In winter time it was knitted woollen

Dinton school c. 1904

hats, scarves and gloves and muffs in which on cold days my mother would put a hot potato to keep my hands warm, and my brother had one in his overcoat pocket. There was no central heating in church or schools, so we were allowed to keep our coats on during school hours.

Lou Winters saw many of the old families pass away. Her brother was killed in the First World War and her fiancé in the Second. She witnessed the return of troops from Dunkirk as they moved around the streets of Dinton with little more than their trousers and odd boots to wear. The villagers gave willing hospitality to them as well as to the families who fled the bombing in London.

But there were many occasions for communal enjoyment. Chief among the national and seasonal

right] An immaculately turned out company of American servicemen stationed at the new depôt at Dinton during the 2nd World War. These 'hangars' can still be seen behind houses, where they formed part of the now closed RAF Chilmark. The depôt was built to supply the American army and air force with equipment for D Day and after.

The Dinton Bonfire Boys, 1890-95. Holding the cane on the left is Smith, coachman at Compton House. In the centre, wearing a bowler hat, is George Cuff. George Stacey, also with bowler, is second from right.

celebrations recorded in the village annals are the activities of the Dinton Bonfire Boys on 5 November. Since the end of the 19th century and possibly before, a torchlight procession led by a banner-holder and the Dinton Brass Band, toured the entire parish including the hamlets of Baverstock and Hurdcott. They returned to the centre for a bonfire built almost entirely from faggots donated by local farmers. Two appointed clowns fringed the procession to jolly up the proceedings.

Changes wrought by war, and the preparations for war, were to stamp themselves as indelibly on the face of Dinton as they had on Chilmark. In 1937 the brickyard closed down. One young boy, desperate to witness the demolition of the huge kiln chimney, persuaded his mother to write a letter to his school at Wilton saying that he was sick. This was fine until the following week when the Salisbury Journal published a photograph of the demolition with the young pupil in front. Mr Eliot, the Wilton School headmaster would not have been amused! At the same time RAF Dinton was created with responsibilities for the new ammunition depot at Chilmark Quarry. This proved helpful as many of the brickyard workers were able to obtain fresh employment. From 1943 to 1944 the huge storage hangars, still visible today, were erected by the Americans on land bordering the railway.

The American influx was considerable, as camps existed at Tisbury, Teffont and in Dinton Park making quite an impression on the local society. Continuous jazz music from

Members of the Dinton Methodist Chapel around 1931

Dinton Park, for example, upset the vicar whose sermons could not be heard, but the blacksmith did not complain. He developed a prosperous extension to his business, selling and repairing bicycles for Yanks who had not seen them before but soon recognised them as the ideal transport for

Moving from the old American air force Nissen huts at Dinton after the 2nd World War. They had provided accommodation for young couples from the village who could not find homes. Gladys Gipson said that a whole new generation of Dinton babies was born there. From left to right: Mrs Kelly and daughter (Mr Clayton behind), Jim Gipson and daughter, Mr and Mrs Scammell and daughter.

rural life. Relations were generally good and five of the local girls later left the village as GI brides.

Although the camps disappeared at the war's end, they left at least two legacies. The hangars remained as storage for propellant fuel and for many years American Army Nissen huts near Fourways provided homes for local people. First to move into one was the postmistress, Gladys Gipson:

> I met my husband while the RAF camp was being built. He came down from London to work there about 1936. As wages clerk he visited the post office to collect insurance stamps for the hundreds of men working there. After the war we got married. He went to work at the station but we had no home. The chairman of the parish council, Colonel Perkins, was trying to get the Nissen huts taken over for the young people of the village to live in as there were no houses for us. At that time people were squatting wherever they could and strangers could not have been evicted so my husband and I went early one morning and moved in. When other young couples saw what we had done they soon followed suit. A whole generation of Dinton babies was born there!

The closure of Dinton station in 1966 caused surprisingly little protest. Bus services through the valley were good and traffic in local produce had declined to such an extent that the rest was easily conveyed by road. With the decay of the old agricultural community there came a rash of new building estates as Dinton took on its modern form. Nevertheless, it has suffered less than many other villages. It retains its school, its pub, a vineyard and a busy industrial estate. The shop-cum-post office, imaginatively run, is as lively as ever. There remains about the village an air of pleasant rural existence. A G Street, the Wilton farmer, broadcaster and writer, summed it up rather well, as his daughter Pamela recalls in her *Portrait of Wiltshire*:

> When I was young 'going for a drive' was still one of those gentler innocuous forms of pleasure undertaken by the family at regular intervals. Almost invariably we ended up at

Dinton ladies cricket team

Marshwood. 'Lovely place,' my father would say stopping
the car. Gently but firmly my mother would remind him of
the domestic difficulties of living without neighbours,
shops, or buses for miles around. 'But that's the beauty of
it,' my father would remark shaking his head and starting
up the car again, gazing regretfully at the isolated grey stone
farmhouse as we drove slowly by until such times the urge
to see Marshwood overtook him once more.

Marshwood, a late-Georgian farmhouse to the north
of the village was once the home of Edward Whatmore, who
patented a movable fire escape which could also be used for
fruit picking. It remains today, a working farm in its
beautiful downland setting, as a reminder of a far less
frantic era and the dreams of a local farmer.

10

Baverstock
an Enchanting Route to
Grovely

Though no Toll Gate stood at the entrance to Baverstock, a
symbolic barrier shut out the hazardous, unknown world
beyond.

Staying with the Aunts Ida Gandy

Y OU COULD VERY EASILY miss Baverstock as you
pass through the Nadder Valley at a point where
the railway bisects the B3089. If so, it would be
your loss. From the small 14th-century church, prominent
on a grassy knoll, a single meandering lane past picturesque
cottages and an ancient manor presents a scene of great

The home of Patrick Faithfull –
the only surviving agricultural
worker to live in the village.
His home lies just before the
track that disappears into
Grovely Woods. Note the
examples of bygone farming
tools still displayed on the
wall.

tranquillity. It is fringed by streams and spring flowers and
peters out to the merest track into the ancient woodland of
Grovely . You may even encounter the bearded figure of
Patrick Faithfull, with wide-brimmed cowboy hat, cantering
his Irish draught-horse across the fields. Patrick has spent
forty years of his working life on the Dinton and Baverstock
farms. His cottage, the last you will encounter, has a
conservatory like a birdcage (once a kiosk at the Tinkerbell
Garage!) and a garden in which rusting antique farm
implements blend with the roses. Despite the nostalgia
aroused by his surroundings, he has no illusions about the
past. He has seen agriculture move from the muscle-
straining days that his horses symbolise to the high-tech
mechanisation of today and sheds few tears at its passing:

right] Baverstock Manor. A
smaller, earlier part of the
present residence was in the
possession of Wilton Abbey. It
was used as a retreat for the
nuns and as a hostel for
visiting pilgrims. The present
building is believed to have
been completed in Jacobean
times.

> If you've worked out in the fields every day with horses
> when it's pouring down with rain and the mud's up to the

top of your boots – then you get in a modern trailer cab and see which one you prefer!

Baverstock is a long, narrow wedge of land between Dinton and Barford St Martin. Bounded by Grovely Woods to the north, it runs down to the Nadder where it embraces the manor of Hurdcott shrouded by woodland. W H Saumarez Smith, in his scholarly work *A History of Baverstock,* emphasises the strong links that existed with the Abbey at Wilton. In AD 955, a gift of land given to the abbey by King Edgar included three hides (about 300 acres) at Baverstock. A century later, the Domesday Book shows 'Babestocke' still within the possession of the abbey. Later, in the 15th century, a small house was built there for the newly elected abbess, Cecilia Willoughby, whose family continued to be associated with the village for the next hundred years. It was used as a retreat for the nuns as well as a hostel for visiting pilgrims. The house was situated near St Mary's Well, a spring of pure water supposedly possessed of mystic healing powers. This small residence formed the earliest part of the present manor house believed to have been completed in Jacobean times.

Over the centuries, little would have disturbed the rustic peace of Baverstock outside the normal rhythm of the agricultural year. In earlier times, the ancient droveway to the north of the village took travellers to and from the cathedral city of Salisbury and the 18th-century turnpike (now the B3089) transported the new coach traffic to the west. Even the laying of the Salisbury to Exeter line in 1859 caused only temporary disturbance as the nearest station was at Dinton. In such a quiet community the discovery of a highwaywoman in their midst must have come as a great shock!

On a spring afternoon in 1779, a Mrs Thring was walking along the toll road about half a mile from her home at Burcombe. A person on horseback dressed as a man drew up beside her. After a short conversation he drew a pistol and demanded her property. Mrs Thring reluctantly handed over 2s and a black silk cloak. The stranger then demanded her ring and shoebuckles. At this, Mrs Thing falsely declared her husband to be in sight. The thief then took fright and rode off.

When she arrived home, Mrs Thring immediately raised the alarm. Her assailant was overtaken and captured quite easily. Although the pistol had been thrown over a hedge, there was plenty of incriminating evidence and the thief was arrested. Closer examination showed – to the astonishment of all – that the prisoner was not only female, but a 24-year-old lady from Baverstock known to them all. Mary Abraham, *alias* Mary Sandall, was committed to Fisherton Gaol. At the July assizes in Salisbury she was sentenced to death, although her sentence was later commuted.

In 1796 the old rectory adjacent to the church burnt down. It was replaced in 1823 by the residence we see now opposite the church, aptly described by Mr Saumarez Smith as 'a gracious and commodious house, suitable for a Regency Rector in comfortable circumstances'. It was built for the largely absentee rector, Richard Hitchens, who enjoyed it for only four years before his death.

His successor, William Hony, was to remain for the rest of his life – forty-eight years. He was responsible, not only for the first radical restoration of the church, at that time in a wretched condition, but for Baverstock's only school, built on the site of the old rectory.

Baverstock

Baverstock church fronted by war graves of Australian soldiers erected by the Imperial War Graves Commission in 1924. There are 32 of them, and would have included those who died from the virulent 'flu epidemic in 1918. Nearby Hurdcott House had been the headquarters of No. 3 Command Depot of the Australian Imperial Force and later used partly as a military hospital.

There he taught regularly and added a bakehouse to the building so that the girls could learn breadmaking.

William Hony, described as 'a handsome man with a benign but authoritative air', became Archdeacon of Sarum and a Residentiary Canon of Salisbury Cathedral. His five daughters are vividly portrayed by their niece, Ida Gandy, in her book *Staying with the Aunts* which mentions their idyllic childhood at Baverstock. Life centred on their garden and the cultivation of the glebe land, a passion they shared with their father. Hay making was the most exciting event of the year and, in winter, skating on Dinton Pond. Tea parties were the great social events heightened by the arrival of croquet in mid-19th century with 'ices, claret and cider cup and tea, and then a cold collation with champaign [*sic*] at 7 o'clock'.

One joy shared by all in the village was timeless:

Beyond the garden and the glebe the place dearest to my Aunts was Grovely Wood, set on a hillside a mile or so north of their home. For them it was enchanted ground, and as I read of their affection for it I remembered the low intense voice which Aunt Margaret used whenever she spoke of it. In the Wood grew the sweetest white violets in all England; the finest hazels; its nightingales were the most musical. The villagers, too, appreciated the Wood and swarmed there to pick the nuts. Once my grandfather found all the cottages empty on a fine September afternoon because everyone was nutting (and small wonder since low wages could be supplemented by selling the result at 12s a sack).

The path to Grovely crosses the Ox Drove and leads to Grovely Lodge. Once a thriving woodland village for estate workers existed here complete with its own church. This was taken down stone by stone when a previous benefactor emigrated to Australia. Now nothing remains but a few scattered dwellings.

The villagers of Baverstock would have returned from their nutpicking to cottages that were damp and often overcrowded. They would have lacked ventilation and proper sanitation. It is no wonder that illness was a regular occurrence. Today their homes are barely recognisable. Hidden behind 20th-century exteriors or gathered together to form more commodious cottages, they have gone upmarket. It seems that Patrick Faithfull is the only agricultural labourer left to represent the centuries-old preoccupation with the land.

Hurdcott House, early last century. The hamlet of Hurdcott until recent times had always been part of the ecclesiastical parish of Baverstock, which was united with Barford in 1884. During the 1st World War Hurdcott House became the headquarters of No. 3 command Depot of the Australian Imperial Force. Many sick and wounded soldiers returned there from the front.

11

Barford

By the Ford of St Martin

MANY MOTORISTS will be familiar with Barford
St Martin. It is the point where the B3089
meets the broad curve of the A30 as it sweeps
round from Wilton and crosses the Nadder at Gall Bridge.
Here, flocks of sheep graze peacefully along the flood plain
of the Nadder. After heavy rain the channels of the old water
meadows are still clearly defined.

Evidence of early settlement can be seen along the
southern boundary of Grovely Woods. The earthworks
known as Hamshill (or Hamsel) Ditches are the remains of
a large native village occupied throughout the Roman period
and having its origin in the Iron Age. In the valley, too,

development would have occurred at quite an early stage. As the name implies, the village grew by the ford of St Martin, the patron saint of the church.

The main part of the village clusters around the church near the crossroads known locally as Four Corners. St Martin's Church, cruciform in shape, was built in the early 13th century and has a 15th-century battlemented tower in the Perpendicular style. The oldest part of the church is the chancel. It contains a rather unusual Elizabethan tomb recessed in the south wall with a painted figure of a woman lying on a reed mattress. The stained glass, however, is modern; the windows behind the altar were dedicated in 1919 'in thankfulness for a brother returned from the War'. All were donated by the Dawkins family, still represented in the village today.

Barford

left] Scene looking west along Barford village street, early last century, with St Martin's church, churchyard and village cross (behind the standing men)

below] Thomas Dawkins, c.1904. His family were builders in the village and seem to have included wealthy benefactors to the church.

In the south chapel of this beautifully kept church is a fine brass dedicated in 1584 to Alis Walker: 'Thomas Walker her eldest sonne in token of his love and duty hath erected this monument.' She is shown kneeling before a book with her eleven children, all in Elizabethan dress. Just to the left is a large squint, enabling worshippers in the side chapel to see the altar.

In the narrow lane fronting the church there is a limestone village cross though, like so many, it has lost in the course of time much of its original shape. Its age is uncertain. Ancient tradition suggests that it is older than the church itself and possibly succeeds a wooden cross placed there by early missionaries as a preaching station.

East End Farm, on the busy A30, remains part of the Pembroke Estate. An earlier residence here, known as 'The House of Ball', is believed to be where pilgrims would call in pre-Dissolution times to obtain tickets of admission to Wilton Abbey. In 1900 a disastrous fire destroyed many of the outbuildings but the farmhouse was saved by the resourcefulness of Harry Dawkins, a local carpenter.

Jack Combes was born at the Manor Farm in 1908, a few years after the fire at East End Farm, but his family was associated with both:

My parents were disappointed to have a second boy when they wanted a girl. Accordingly I was dressed in frocks and had long ringlets. Mr Clark, the barber, cycled out from Salisbury and I remember sitting in a high chair in the courtyard having my hair cut short. My brother and I were taught at home by a governess, Miss Mangin, who was very kind to us. I later went to a small private school in Wilton, the Moat House in North Street. This was during the First World War when the road from Wilton to Fovant was being reconstructed to take all the heavy traffic to the army camps in Fovant. It was nearly impossible to walk along the road, so we went across the fields. If the weather was bad we were taken by pony trap to Dinton Station to catch the train to Wilton.

Jack worked East End Farm until his retirement. His papers present a very detailed picture of the physical endurance expected of agricultural labourers before mechanisation transformed the local economy:

My father farmed land on the Pembroke Estate. He employed about twelve workers – [including] six carters who arrived at 6 am to feed the ten horses. They then went home for breakfast in their cottages close to the farm returning to start work again from 7 am until 5 pm six days a week. There were three shepherds who looked after about 600 sheep. There were no fences on the downs, so they had to be up there with their dogs to prevent the sheep from straying. The lambing pens were on the hill. They were made of hurdles covered in straw. Lambing of these pedigree Hampshire Down sheep took place in December and January, and was a very cold experience at night in winter.

Three general labourers were employed around the farm as well as a groom/gardener. The carters with their horses did all the work – ploughing, sowing, harrowing, rolling and harvesting. There were two dairies, one with 20 cows, looked after by a dairyman and his wife who lived in Arnold's Cottage where I now live; the other with 40 cows in Dairy Road at the far end of the village. The water meadows were properly irrigated and the cows were put out to grass there on 20 March each year.

Ploughing was hard work for men and horses – usually with a single furrow plough with two horses. On the very heavy land this did not go deep enough, so after the first ploughing the men with the steam plough were engaged to go deeper. This consisted of two steam traction engines, one at either end of the field. A six-furrow plough was attached with a hawser. The engines then pulled it up and down the field.

Barford

Shire horses at Barford St Martin around 1918. Fred Miles, Fred Penny and Frank Daniels are the carters.

Although 17th century in origin, the Barford Inn has been stylishly altered to suit the requirements of the age. It was previously known as the Dragon, or the Green Dragon, and is even claimed to be immortalised by Charles Dickens in his book *Martin Chuzzlewit* as the Blue Dragon. (However, it should be said that the Green Dragon at Alderbury makes a better claim!) In the 19th century it was much used as a coach house mainly for local traffic; the courtyard still houses the old mounting block used to assist horse riders at that time. During the Second World War, the Wiltshire Yeomanry dedicated one of their tanks to the inn, with 'The Green Dragon' inscribed on one side and 'Barford St Martin' on the other.

At all times, the inn has provided an important centre for village social activity. The Green Dragon Slate Club, for example, was a protection society common to most villages from the mid-19th century until the introduction of the National Insurance Act in 1911. It was the only support most

A crumpled memory of the Dragon Inn, later the Green Dragon and now Barford Inn, early last century

right] Anna Dawkins, the Barford midwife from 1905 to 1921. Loved by her patients, she walked considerable distances to see them day and night, often without the aid of a doctor. If the family were poor she would take home washing to do with the aid of her ten children. Today her descendants still live in the village.

villagers could hope for against the worst effects of misfortune. Through the weekly subscriptions of its members, it ensured a means of support when doctors' fees or funeral expenses had to be paid. It also provided a bond of fellowship in an area of activity where trade union organisation was particularly weak.

One of the most memorable of village holidays was the Slate Club Annual Feast Day. Each Whit Monday a parade assembled at Barford Rectory. It was headed by two men carrying the heavy club banner, a green silk emblem displaying a painted dragon. The inevitable village band joined the procession which was led by the rector as it made its way to the church for a 10 am service. This was followed by a noisy perambulation of the village. At 1 pm a sumptuous lunch was provided at the Green Dragon Club Room and, later, tea on the lawn of Manor Farm. The day would conclude with dancing outside the inn with

Grovely Lodge in Grovely Wood. This is all that remains of the village that once included a church and its own school.

numerous stalls for amusements and refreshment. Not surprisingly, such events were often accompanied by complaints of drunkenness and excessive high spirits.

One person essential to the village community before medical care was properly established, was the local midwife. Barford St Martin was fortunate in having Anna Dawkins who dedicated herself to this work from 1905 to 1921. She walked miles to see her patients in Barford and the surrounding villages, day and night, often working without the aid of a doctor. If the family she was attending were poor she would take home their washing and complete it with the aid of her ten children. Her many kindnesses were not forgotten. On her retirement the village presented her with an armchair and a framed list of grateful subscribers.

Grovely was the only Wiltshire forest to be mentioned by name in Domesday. Originally part of a much larger area of woodland stretching westwards, by 1603 it had shrunk to fourteen coppices between the villages of the Nadder and the Wylye, predominantly between Barford St Martin and Great Wishford. The inhabitants of both had forest rights including the gathering of dead wood, removing boughs at certain times and felling one load of live wood each year. The annual Oakapple Day festivities at Great Wishford still celebrate these rights. Barford, too, in former days, danced in procession to Salisbury Cathedral making their claim with the words 'Grovely, Grovely, Grovely'.

In 1812, however, Barford appears to have bartered their rights to the live wood, receiving instead from the Lord of the Manor, Lord Pembroke, an annual sum of £5 Bough Money. In the mid-19th century the lord at that time, concerned about the effect on his game, challenged the remaining right to gather dead wood and forbade it. Although the men of the village appear to have accepted this edict meekly enough, the women did not. Fanny Pomeroy, Ann Hibberd, Sarah Abraham and Grace Hibberd challenged the order by going into the forest and gathering their load. They were summoned before the local magistrates, fined and on their refusal to pay, were imprisoned. The following day, the village right to gather dead wood was confirmed. Not even Lord Pembroke could take it away. The women were released and fêted for their courage. Grace Hibberd (later Read) continued to live on in the village until her death at ninety-one.

The stone mason, Edwin Rixon, has appeared before in our valley story. Having spent his earlier life in Tisbury

above] An unknown inhabitant of Barford, early 20th century

left] Grace Read (née Hibberd) outside her cottage, now Primrose Cottage. As a girl of 13, she was one of four women imprisoned in defence of the villagers' ancient rights in Grovely Wood. She died aged 91 in 1898. She could remember the rejoicings after the Battle of Waterloo and liked to tell of how an ox was roasted whole in the village to celebrate the conclusion of hostilities.

and Chilmark, he arrived at Barford St Martin in 1924. Fairholme, his home and small-holding for the rest of his life, still survives at the western end of the village. Like most other villagers, he had good reason to be grateful to the staunch women who had protected his rights. The collection of 'snappings', or faggot wood, provided the only source of heat for his family warming their cottage and enabling them to cook domestically as well as to prepare their animal feed in an outhouse copper. Almost until he died in 1954, he and his wife Emma took frequent trips to Grovely to collect wood with the assistance of two handcarts, which they secured to themselves with straps. Rixon's diaries show a daily preoccupation with the domestic arrangements of his household. They clearly show a high degree of self-sufficiency which must have existed within rural cottage life right up to and including the Second World War.

Joe Chalke lived to the age of ninety five, spending nearly all his life in Barford. A descendant of woodmen going back to the seventeenth century, he was a spar and hurdle maker who knew Grovely as well as anyone. He left school at twelve and worked with his father, Harry, who had a smallholding as well as a wood and coal business. In addition, their contract to repair the roads around the village meant frequent visits to the Great Western Railway station at Wilton to collect cartloads of stone. Joe's other duties included looking after his father's cows and carthorses, sowing corn by hand and then cutting it with a scythe.

Following service in the Royal Marines from 1914 to 1921, Joe and his wife Vi, had a dairy at Ugford, delivering milk to Wilton during the twenties and thirties. He was a regular member of the Barford Football Club playing his last game for them at the age of fifty-six! During the Second World War he turned to carpentry and continued in the construction industry until his retirement at sixty-nine. He then returned to the craft he had inherited from his ancestors. Until his death in 1991 he was still visiting Grovely regularly, cutting wood from the hazel coppices for the hurdles and spars he made so dexterously.

The foundations of Barford St Martin's first council houses were laid in 1946 on a site in Dairy Road, north of the railway line. Since that time a large estate has developed.

The old Barford St Martin
bridge with Jesse Avery, born
1893, from Four Winds

Further infilling of private dwellings throughout the village
has been fairly well controlled although the busyness of the
A30 and B3089 detracts from the air of rural calm. The
school, founded in 1854, when Charles Nicholson
bequeathed money to fund a schoolmaster as well as tools
for apprentices and uniforms for housemaids, is still
functioning. Gall Bridge, however, the narrow hump-backed
bridge which crossed the Barley Ford, was swept away
during a severe storm in 1980 and replaced with the rather
featureless structure we see today.

12

Ansty
the St John's Hospitallers

HAVING COMPLETED our journey along the northern flank of the Nadder, we must return to the rivers source in the Donheads and the line of tiny villages that nestle almost secretively among wooded coombs off the A30. The original road, the Upper Herepath, ran along the top of the downland to the south. Turnpiked for a short while in 1762, it had long formed part of the main London to Exeter route before descending precipitously down White Sheet Hill. Here, it joined the present road at the Glove Inn (now Arundell Farm) where extra teams of horses were kept to assist those travelling in the opposite direction towards Salisbury.

In 1895 men from Ansty were among those who excavated a new road. It zigzagged down the steep ridge providing a route from Alvediston in the Ebble Valley, through their village to the railhead at Tisbury. Ansty remains one of the loveliest villages in the Nadder Valley. Its centre of spring-fed duckpond, church, inn (now a private residence) and manor house present a model of rural tranquillity. To the north, through scattered cottages, many still thatched, tiny streams from the village and the hamlet of Ansty Coomb meet at Ansty Water and flow onwards to the Nadder at Tisbury. Village associations with Crusaders, clandestine marriages and the tallest free-standing maypole in England provide a history that is just as romantic.

In AD 890, King Alfred is reputed to have hunted here through a valley still heavily wooded. After the Norman Conquest the manor passed to the Turberville family who, in 1211, gave it to the Order of Knights Hospitallers – possibly a political expedient. King John's insistence on appointing his own Archbishop of Canterbury had led to his excommunication and a papal interdict. All English churches were closed from 1208 to 1214. This did not apply to the two Crusader Orders of Hospitallers and Templars. Thus, at Ansty, the court was provided with a religious centre when hunting in the surrounding royal forests.

The Order of Knights Hospitallers arose from the first crusade of 1099. It evolved from the work of the Benedictine brothers of the ancient hospice of St John the Almoner in Jerusalem. Here they provided hospitality, care and protection to Christian pilgrims. When the Crusaders were pushed out of the Holy Land, the order moved from Cyprus to Rhodes and finally to Malta.

In England the hospitallers were grouped into local administrative units known as commanderies with about one in each county. The Commandery at Ansty is reputedly the most complete survival in England. When Richard II reaffirmed their possessions at Ansty, his charter referred to a hermitage with eight dwellings. Today we can still see their church completed in 1230 and fragments of the commander's house in the manor (almost totally rebuilt after the Reformation). The large barn-like structure known today as the

The medieval Commandery of the Order of the Knights Hospitallers at Ansty overlooking its fish pond

Commandery is believed to have been the first indoor riding school in the country, possibly on the site of the hospice for the care of travellers and the sick. All these surround the fish pond unusually constructed at a higher level than the road. It has a water-wheel at one end that in living memory pumped fresh water to neighbouring farms and the village.

For three hundred years the order remained at Ansty caring for the physical and spiritual needs of pilgrims journeying along the ridgeway from Salisbury to Shaftesbury. The hospitallers gave medical assistance to the royal keepers and hunting parties of Cranborne Chase. They also provided help to the quarrymen and masons seeking out and preparing stone for the building of Salisbury Cathedral and many other local churches. Although finally dissolved by Henry VIII as part of the suppression of the monasteries, the order was revived in 1831 and survives today in the work of the St John Ambulance Brigade. In 1961 their 750th anniversary was celebrated at Ansty when a procession of the order, clad in their black cloaks with one eight-pointed star on the left breast, joined members of the present-day St John Ambulance Brigade for a service in the church.

The crusader church of St James, one of the few built by the order, is surmounted by three stone crosses each with two horizontal arms, the patriarchal cross of the hospitallers. It is unusual in having a nave and chancel of almost equal proportions. Within the chancel there are carved Caroline stalls brought from Salisbury Cathedral at the end of the 18th century to replace the ageing stalls used by the hospitallers. These had been screened off from the nave which served in those days as the parish church of the village. The blue and gold cloth hanging behind the altar was purchased from Westminster Abbey after the coronation of Queen Elizabeth II in 1953.

After the dissolution, the manor of Ansty was purchased by Sir Francis Zouch who sold it ten years later to the Arundells at Wardour. The Arundells remained patrons of the church for the next three hundred years but, being Roman Catholics, were prevented by statute from presenting vicars. The living was, therefore, a 'donative benefice', given as a gift, and not under the authority of the Bishop of Salisbury who was unable to direct payment of tithes for the maintenance of the church. Its upkeep was often neglected. It gained a reputation for clandestine marriages and other irregularities which the bishop was helpless to suppress. In 1898, however, donative benefices

right] A new Ansty maypole, culled from Wardour Woods, being erected in 1962. Its 1982 successor, from Fonthill Park, was snapped off by a storm in 1993, so that the present maypole dates from 1994 and is only half as tall.

were abolished and a vicar, the Rev. Quartus Bacon, was legally appointed for the first time since the Reformation.

The origins of Ansty Maypole, once the tallest in England, and its annual celebrations are reputed to go back to pagan times commemorating the coming of spring. A more feasible tradition is that the maypole was first erected by the Arundells in the 16th century when tenants of the estate brought their children to be introduced to one another. It has remained continuously since then, apart from 1644 to 1660 when Puritan influence removed it by government statute.

Ansty Maypole is replaced every twenty years or so, always with a silver coin placed beneath the weather vane. The previous one, a Douglas Fir erected in 1982, was some 98 ft

out of the ground, the tallest in the country. It came from Fonthill Park, unlike its predecessors which had always been felled in Wardour Woods. In December 1993 disaster struck when high winds brought it crashing to the ground. A hasty search was made to ensure a new one would be in place before the 1994 May Day and eventually a suitable replacement was purchased in Wales. For reasons of safety, this one is a mere 50 ft above ground but is guaranteed to last for at least forty years.

The pole stands prominently in the centre of the village just north of the pond. It is at a junction with the Ansty Coomb road that passes the old Maypole inn, previously an excellent hostelry known in earlier days as the Arundell Arms. By tradition, a new pole must be in place between sunrise and sunset of a single day otherwise the right to have it in the road is forfeited.

right] Ansty Band at Lower Farm early in the 20th century. It was known to be one of the finest in the area.

The late Cyril Feltham, whose family is one of the few still represented in the village, recorded his amusing memories of the Ansty May Day celebrations at the beginning of the last century. Written almost as a stream of consciousness, they give an impression of a village letting its hair down in a fashion more earthy and prolonged than is usual today:

Ansty Band met in the morning then marched to the local farms for a drink of cider, some drank more than others. After visiting 6 farms they then marched to Lambert's ground gate to meet the Rev. Quarty's Bacon, who walked across the footpath from Swallowclift (as spelt then) headed by the band and flag bearer Grandfather Charles Feltham marched to Ansty Church for 9.30 am service. Henry Feltham fell asleep as the Vicar preached the sermon giving May Day blessings he woke up and shouted Yer! Yer! thinking he was at the club dinner, held in the barn at the Arundell Arms.

After the dinner speeches and songs, the festivities began, outside the band seated in a farm waggon played for dancing. Wardour school children, in care of the Sisters who learnt

them, danced round the maypole gracefully Stalls each side of the road leading to the pub, such as Mrs Weldon, famous for her gingerbreads ½d each and brandy balls ½d each, also swinging boats 1 penny a ride increasing to 2 pennies in the evening, and coconut shies 3 balls for sixpence. Stainers selling various items, Humbys sweets and cakes home made. Confettie and water squirts ½d a bag, ½d a squirt, the water squirted inside the girls' blouses, then the confettie put down made it stick well.

Over the other side of the wall in the field opposite the pole, the swinging boats and James Birchall's tent with 2 compartments, one side was a silent film, the other a shooting gallery. Outside he had a big brass drum he beat and shouted come and have a shoot at my cock 3 pence a shot, which meant, inside on a long stick attached to the top on a swivel, was a cockerell made of tin, if you hit it, it would spin round.

right] Ansty House opposite the pond. All the workshops (notice the clock and bell) were removed in the early 1950s, and only the house remains. It was previously the home of Charles Edgar Lever and his brother Walt, who were wheelwrights and carpenters.

left] Ansty Band, early 20th century. Seven members belonged to either the Parsons or Feltham families, who are still represented in the village.

Then towards evening and darkness beginning to fall the band formed outside the pub and followed by the crowd marched round the pole to the tune; 'The Oyster Gal', known to the locals as 'Raw Cabbage and Onions'. They then finished in the pub with a sing song and some of the bandsmen playing their instruments, a good time had by all.

At that time festivities centred on a barn next to the inn but after the First World War Ansty acquired a redundant hut from the vast wartime army camp at nearby Fovant. Erected on land opposite the wood yard and given by the Arundell estate at a peppercorn rent, it became the centre of a thriving village social life. The band was always the hub of such activities attending many of the local Slate Club feasts as well. On one occasion they visited the Beckford Arms at Fonthill Gifford and did not return for a day or so. The landlord, Maurice Benjafield, later reflected admiringly, 'That be a good band. They play just as well on their backs as on their feet!'

The end of the Second World War brought even greater changes, made more dramatic by the break up of the Arundell estate. Ansty's cottages and farms were mostly sold to their tenants at prices that seem unbelievably low today. Employment that had depended on the estate, however, dwindled and the village population with it.

Les Parsons, a recently retired local thatcher, is the fourth generation of his family skilled in this craft and has no one to follow him. One of only three old families still living in the village, he has witnessed the change from a thriving agricultural community to a largely residential retreat:

> My family go back to the mid-19th century in this village. It was mostly smallholdings then with perhaps eight to ten cows. We were estate workers and tenants of several Wardour farms. All the workers had second jobs: stone masons, for example, or thatchers like us, a craft that started with the universal skill of thatching ricks.
>
> I was related to half the village and as we were all Catholics, we walked to school together through the woods to Wardour. When we left there was always work on the estate. William Hansford, the landlord of the Royal Oak at Swallowcliffe, rented the medieval commandery as a

Ansty village party to celebrate the opening of the village hall following the 1st World War

workshop at the beginning of the century and his son
George carried on the business until about 1962. Although
it was primarily a wagon works, they were also undertakers
and did many of the practical jobs about the estate. My
maternal grandfather, Sidney Alford, was the wheelwright
there. One of his sons, James, was the blacksmith and his
brother William was the carpenter.

Christopher Ridley's family has felled the Wardour
Woods for many generations. He continues to run the wood
yard, producing fencing panels and home-grown timber
products. It is the only surviving industrial unit. Ansty is
now a conservation area and its plans for any proposed
development are studied very carefully before permission is
given. This is to ensure that the character of the village is
not spoiled. There are now only fifty-five houses and
residents number around one hundred and two. As with
other Nadder Valley villages, many houses have become
second homes occupied for short periods. Other residents
have stayed briefly – in some cases their houses have seen
three or four owners in ten years. All this has increased
property prices far beyond the reach of many local people.

Jack Feltham, whose family has witnessed all the
changes, considers himself fortunate to be able to continue
living there. He puts the problem in its most pragmatic
form: 'If you want a lovely village, and an active village with
young people, what you need is new building, not keeping it
as it is now. Otherwise you will have a dead village. You
must have balance.'

13

The Cliff of the Swallow

Beyond Lower Farm the fields were all parted with high
hedges which in spring time was a beautiful sight with
thousands of primroses. At Easter we used to pick them in
small bunches with leaves and moss for the church
decorations but eventually the hedges were dug up and the
beauty gone.

Ethel Turner

ETHEL TURNER came to Swallowcliffe in 1896 at the
age of three weeks. Her mother having died in
childbirth, she was taken to live with her
grandmother, Mrs Rixon, in one of the small cottages
opposite the Royal Oak. Within this small cottage, two up
and two down, the Rixons lived for fifty-seven years and

brought up their own family of nine children before Ethel and her brother arrived. With very little heating and the limited light of oil lamps, Mrs Rixon made shirts for men of the village and her husband supplied their families with honey from his numerous hives. Next door, in one small room downstairs, lived Mrs Cross:

[She] only had 5s a week from the Board of Guardians to live on. She used to do dress-making working half the night with the aid of a small oil lamp or candles. My grandmother always gave her a Sunday lunch and sometimes in the week if Mrs Cross had a good week at sewing, she would send me to shop for a small tin of salmon which was 6d and always asked that Mr Spencer opened it for her. From this she would make fish cakes with potatoes. Once a year at Easter she washed all the choir surplices from church using the water the potatoes had been cooked in for starch. She also cleaned the school and church.

The shop run by Tom Spencer and his family in High Street, Swallowcliffe, early 20th century

Much that we know of the history of Swallowcliffe comes from the researches of the late Commander Stephen Jenkins. In 1953 he moved to Vine Cottage where he discovered in his garden, fragments of early pottery. The curator of Salisbury Museum was able to confirm them as being of Roman and Norman origin. Fired with enthusiasm by this discovery, Stephen Jenkins spent the rest of his long retirement investigating every aspect of village development from the early settlements on Ansty and Swallowcliffe Downs to the last vestiges of the declining agricultural community in the mid-20th century.

In 1966 one of the most exciting archaeological finds in the Nadder Valley, that of a richly furnished burial site, was made on Swallowcliffe Down. It was discovered in an early Bronze Age barrow which had been reused in the 7th century. It contained a young female, possibly an Anglo-Saxon princess, aged eighteen to twenty-five years, lying on an elaborate ashwood bed with iron fittings. Although the grave had been disturbed and probably robbed in the 19th century, it still contained much of interest including domestic utensils and elaborate ornaments of the period.

The name Swallowcliffe is first recorded in an Anglo-Saxon charter of AD 940, when King Edmund gave to his thegn, Garulf, nine measures of land 'in that place which the

Swallowcliffe

left] An early flying machine in a field above Swallowcliffe Wood in September 1910. This Farman aeroplane was one of several to be seen around south Wiltshire during the military manoeuvres which took place at that time. Flown regularly by Captain Bertram Dickson, this bi-plane was powered by a 7-cylinder French-built Gnome engine. Its top speed was just 50 mph.

country people jokingly call "the cliff of the swallow", that is Swealewan cif'. The charter goes on to outline the village boundaries, which seem very little changed to this day. There is also a stern warning from King Edmund that if anyone should attempt to interfere with his gift to Garulf, 'let him be punished with the frozen blasts of glaciers, and with the winged army of malignant spirits, unless first he amends himself with whole-hearted penitence'.

By 1066 much of the village had passed to Wilton Abbey and subsequently, at the time of the Reformation, to the Pembrokes. It was more than the physical presence of Choulden Hill that separated Swallowciffe from its neighbouring parish of Ansty. One was Protestant Pembroke and the other Catholic Arundell but relationships between them appear to have been amicable. The only recorded conflict was their common objections, often manifested with cowhorns, bells and other instruments, towards the later dissenter chapels!

Between 1803 and 1811, the architect John Buckler was commissioned by Sir Richard Colt Hoare to make a record of Wiltshire churches for his library at Stourhead. They are skilfully drawn, giving a remarkable insight into the appearance of many churches before Victorian restoration dramatically changed them.

Fortunately, Buckler's drawings include one of the original 12th-century church of St Peter, Swallowcliffe, which stood at a junction just east of the Royal Oak. It shows a substantial building with an embattled tower above the porch. In 1750 the churchyard, surrounded by rails, was recorded as the point at which Lord Pembroke's tenants met on 20 June to walk the bounds of the summer fields.

The position of St Peter's by a stream amidst water meadows was not an ideal site. By the 18th century the church had sunk to such a point that frequent flooding was suffered 'to a level above the seats sometimes leaving mud an inch thick on them'. A decision was finally taken to replace it, a task that was completed in only thirteen months ready for the consecration of the new church by the Bishop of Salisbury on 29 August 1843.

The new St Peter's Church, built on a higher site, was one of the first to be designed by the celebrated Victorian architect Gilbert Scott. It was intended to model the original from which much of its re-tooled stone is believed to have come. The 14th-century stone effigy of a knight was also removed from the old church and placed in the porch of the new. It is believed to be that of Sir Thomas West who endowed a chantry at St John's Hospital, Wilton, thus providing a chaplain to say daily mass for himself and other favoured villagers. There is also a mystery in the porch. A clear indentation can be seen where a brass has been removed. The Monumental Brass Society believe it to have been that of an abbess holding a crozier over her right shoulder. A number of such brasses were originally taken from Wilton and Shaftesbury Abbeys after the dissolution and apparently placed in small churches for safe keeping. But where is it now?

Swallowcliffe Manor, the oldest building in the village, stands imposingly to the east of Common Lane. Built in the 17th century on the site of a much older building, it was constructed of ashlar with handsome, mullioned windows and a roof of sturdy ship's timbers. The manor was originally a farmhouse. A beautifully drafted 'illuminated address' presented by the villagers in 1907 to William Keevil, the last farmer to live there, is topped by a drawing of the building as it was at that time. Later, the north wing was rebuilt by Capt. Henry Cavendish, the new owner and a cousin of the Duke of Devonshire, using red brick faced with the local Chilmark stone.

Long established in the fabric of Swallowcliffe society was the Wright family. They served the community as tanners, cordwainers (shoemakers), wheelwrights, shopkeepers

Swallowcliffe

Swallowcliffe church early this century. The manor house can be seen in the background.

and publicans over several recorded centuries. It was a John Wright, for example, who purchased a parcel of land and extended the old tannery to a building which is now the Royal Oak. One of the chimney stacks of this building still bears the date 1705. Four generations of the family continued the tannery business until the 1850s when it became the attractive inn we see today. With its steep-

The Royal Oak at Swallowcliffe, 1907. The landlord, William Hansford, seen outside his inn, also ran a carpentry and wheelwright business, repairing farm and commercial machinery from the Commandery at Ansty.

pitched thatched roof and stone mullioned windows it is little changed externally and is still referred to occasionally by local residents as the tanyard. William Hansford, the builder and wheelwright from Ansty, had become the landlord there by 1903 as well as continuing his active workshop at the old commandery at Ansty. Followed by his son George, the family managed the Royal Oak for over half a century.

Another old inn, converted from a farmhouse, was the London Elm. It existed as one of a row of cottages, covered with red and yellow roses, along the dusty track of the Salisbury to Shaftesbury road (now the A30). Kelly's Directory shows it to have been closed by 1915. On the downland opposite, the dairy farmer, Maurice Waters, carved in the chalk his own advertisement: 'DRINK MORE MILK'. It is said that when he heard criticisms of this in the London Elm he threatened to add the words 'AND LESS BEER!' The last landlord was Arthur Tanner whose son was killed at Gallipoli. The vicar, Quartus Bacon, refused permission for a monument in his son's honour to be placed in the churchyard. Mrs Tanner was so incensed she went to the Bishop's Palace in the Cathedral Close and confronted the

Swallowcliffe

left] The London Elm Inn on the A30 at Swallowcliffe, which closed about 1915. The haycart had come from Manston, a village between Shaftesbury and Blandford. Notice the narrow width of the A30 at that time.

bishop personally. He agreed to their request and the resulting monument, a symbolic broken pillar, can be seen to the right of the churchyard path.

Today it is easy to forget the importance of such ancient crafts as well-digging when piped water is so much a feature of modern living. In the past, for those living any distance from running water, life could be very difficult without one. Percy Hayter's great grandfather came to Swallowcliffe in 1847. He was employed by the Wilton estate as land-drainer, pond-maker and well-sinker. His importance is indicated by the fact that the estate built him a new house and rented him land to keep a pony which was his only means of transport. Percy was the fourth and last of his family to continue this craft:

> My father never had much faith in water diviners. He despised them. When he was going to make a well, he'd mark out from the centre a 3 ft 6 in radius and dig down till he got some firm soil, maybe 6 feet deep; then he'd go in to 3 ft radius leaving a 6 in ledge all around and build that up with bricks. He'd go on down, working round in a circle like a corkscrew. He'd go down till he found water and he could usually tell how deep he'd have to dig. His opinion was you could find water almost anywhere so it didn't matter where you started digging. Two of us used to sit at the top with a windlass, very strong, and there was a steel cable with a hook and bucket and a seat to bring my father up at the end of the day. There must have been over thirty wells in Swallowcliffe in the old days.

Ethel Turner retained vivid memories of her entire life spent in the village. Her notes revive a community that was not just closely knit but contained characters whose identity was unaffected by commercial or peer-group pressures. The Misses Alford, Ellen and Lucy, for example, were two spinsters of independent means who lived in the High Street and watched the world go by from an upstairs window. Always dressed in long black capes they never missed a service at the nearby church. Mr Hallet drove a tricycle and had a cork arm with a moveable joint. Jack Witt from Barbers Lane lived in a cottage so thick with smoke from his open fire that you could hardly see his blackened face. He caught wild rabbits which he sold to his plentiful customers at 6d each. Odd-job man Roger slept with the horses he loved. He took them to plough down Hacker Lane riding one and leading the other, always with a very short clay pipe which he smoked upside down. James Wright, a boot-maker of local renown, married Anna Lever, a widow, as his second wife but they continued to live in their own cottages.

The sale of the Pembroke lands in 1918 was to affect Swallowcliffe as profoundly as it did many other south Wiltshire villages. The fifteenth Earl was the main landowner in the village possessing 1,000 acres. His family had supported local charities, providing the site for the school and the new St Peter's Church as well as donating funds to build them.

The death of Henry Cavendish in the mid-1920s removed the other aristocratic connection. His wife, Lady

right] Swallowcliffe Post Office around 1928. Ron Hope is the postman with the bicycle. Mary 'Polly' Burt is the postmistress. She performed that role from the end of the 19th century until around the 2nd World War.

Harriet, had died earlier in 1922 having been taken ill at the post office and carried home by milkers on an unhinged gate. They were remembered with affection in the village and the building of the north wing of the manor had provided much needed employment for the local labourers.

The end of the Second World War brought even bigger changes. With the death of Maurice Waters, who had purchased a large portion of the Pembroke land, most of the cottages passed into private hands. Today, Percy Hayter, Ethel Turner and the world they represented have gone. The post office, village shops and the school are all long closed. The remaining labourers' cottages, combined into highly desirable residences, are picturesque reminders of an age now past.

14

Sutton Mandeville
Below the Greensand Hills

T HERE IS A GRIM MESSAGE, obscured by layers of
grime, which has hung in the barn at Sutton
Mandeville Mill for longer than the memories of its
oldest citizens. It warns:

> TAKE NOTE – there are Mantraps and Spring Guns set on
> these premises.

First mentioned in Domesday, surviving fire and
flood, a mill has functioned on this site right up to the 20th
century. Until recently it was a gutted ruin, its machinery
rusting among piles of rifled stone and rotting timbers. In
the autumn of 1994 a new owner converted this desolation

Sutton

Sutton Mandeville mill, early 20th century. After a long period of dereliction, it has recently been rebuilt by the present owner.

into a modern residence.

The mill is one of seven that still stand along the Nadder Valley from Tisbury to Burcombe. Its isolated situation, a good mile from the village centre, lies along a winding lane north of the church. Sutton Mandeville, sheltered by attractive woodland along the upper greensand hills, stretches eastwards from Swallowcliffe to Fovant. Its main street has a secretive air; Church Farm, the Old Schoolhouse, the church, all hidden away on a sheep-grazed knoll, are prosperous reminders of this once busy community. At the western end, the road turns sharply north into Sutton Row where the cottages of farm labourers once marked a gentle descent to the Compasses Inn at Chicksgrove.

The manor of 'South Town' is first recorded as being held by a Geoffrey de Maundeville in the time of Henry I. It

Sutton Mandeville rectory, 1889, with gardeners Bob Cross and Burt Riggs in the foreground. It was built by the Wyndhams of Dinton Park with a view to the Revd John Wyndham, a younger son, succeeding to the living. This he did in 1840.

passed to the Pembrokes after the Reformation but in 1689 both the Sutton and Chicksgrove estates were purchased by the Wyndham family of Dinton House (now Philipps House). Many houses in the area are reminders of the Wyndham connection but the Old Rectory at Sutton Mandeville is by far the largest and the best. It was built in 1833 with a view to the Rev. John Wyndham, a younger son, succeeding to the living. This he did and remained as rector for the next fifty-seven years until his death in 1897 aged eighty-five. During that time he married four times and supervised the restoration of the church as well as the building of the village school.

From All Saints' Church one has a commanding view of the Nadder Valley across pastures still grazed regularly by sheep. Two rectors were convicted of treason during times of religious confusion. The first, John Colyns, was executed by Henry VIII. Later, during the Commonwealth, Thomas

Rosewell was more fortunate, being reprieved by Charles II. The Norman tower of the church, to which a new top was added in 1709, may once have been a watch-tower. Its three bells, like so many others, no longer peal as the structure has weakened. Near the belfry door at the rear of the nave is a striking gravestone engraved with a representation of the Virgin and Child. It lay until recently in the graveyard beneath a yew tree planted in 1780. Among tilting table

Celebration of Queen Victoria's Diamond Jubilee at Sutton Mandeville 1897

tombs can also be seen an unusual column sundial with a ball top. It has three working faces and is marked with the date 1685.

In 1891, when the Census was taken, the Rev. John Wyndham was coming to the end of his long ministry. On a different social footing, the Spensers, Mullins and Grays were all well established families that were to play a prominent part in the changing fortunes of the village throughout the coming century.

Freddie Spenser's grandfather, Edwin, came to the mill as a young apprentice in the 1880s. It was rented at that

left] Revd John Wyndham, rector of Sutton Mandeville for 57 years. During this period he married four times and oversaw the restoration of the church and the building of the school.

time from the Wyndham estate by William Miles, who worked Manor Farm and left the running of the mill to Frank and Louisa Hitchcock. In due course, Edwin Spenser became the miller and after the sale of the Wyndham estate in 1917 he bought the property with its adjacent cottage.

Freddie remembers his grandfather as a tall man, a good foot higher than his wife Elizabeth. A sporty figure with a trilby hat, walking stick and moustache, he had to stoop beneath the low beams of the mill. From 1924, he also managed Manor Farm for William Miles' widow.

Of his two sons, Fred, the younger, remained to learn the trade. The elder, Albert Trulock Spenser, left home in 1924 to manage the Cribbage Hut Inn on the main Salisbury to Shaftesbury road. When the old inn was demolished in 1935, Albert continued as landlord of the stylish new premises, later known as The Lancers, and remained until retirement in 1957.

above] Harry Stone, the Sutton Mandeville pig killer. With him (on the right) are Mr Jukes, the Fovant grocer, and his son – and the latest victim!

left] Fovant Band and villagers outside the old Cribbage Hut Inn, 1920s. The inn stood along the A30 at Sutton Mandeville until 1935, when a new Cribbage Hut, later known as The Lancers, was built further eastwards along the road. The landlord, Albert Trulock Spenser, transferred from the old inn and continued to run the new one until his retirement in 1957.

Freddie Spenser came to live with his grandparents at the mill in 1925:

My first memories are of water everywhere and the old Ford T lorries hauling maize or barley from the railway at Dinton from the docks at Avonmouth. At 2 pm on a Tuesday my father, Fred Spenser, would go to the Salisbury Market House – where the Library is now. He would order cereals which would be at Dinton Station on the 9 o'clock goods train next morning without fail.

At the beginning of the century it was still primarily a flour mill. Deliveries were made all round the area including four bakeries at Tisbury. At one shop in that village each bag had to be carried into the loft. As each sack weighed 240 lbs, it was quite an ordeal. At that time the mill was grinding wheat for flour, barley for animal feed, rolling oats for the horses and cracking beans for sheep. All the cereals came from local farmers until the Twenties when foreign barley could be bought cheaper than English. In addition to supplying bakers, some people came to bake their own bread; there is a very large brick oven at the mill which hasn't been opened in living memory.

From the time flour production ceased in the 1920s, Swallowcliffe Mill went over entirely to animal feed. Most country people had hens in a run to feed and a pig in a sty. This continued until 1937. After that, demand dwindled; the farmers could buy their feed cheaper in bulk. In the end Fred Spenser was buying it from the big firms himself, perhaps 2 to 5 tons at a time:

Sheep shearing at the barn of Manor Farm, Sutton Mandeville on the main A30 road, during the time of William Miles, who farmed there in 1880. His widow was still farming in the 1930s.

Ron Gray lives at Bailey Hill Farm, Sutton Row. He is the third generation of his family to live there. He will show you the scattered entries of his family's issue inscribed in the front pages of an ancient book, Fleetwood's *Life of Christ.* His grandfather, Benedict Gray, was born at Hindon in 1857. By 1891 he had migrated eastwards via Teffont to Sutton Row with his wife, Sarah, and six children. Here he rented 24 acres and the cottage he was later to purchase from the Wyndham estate:

Binder at Sutton Row. Ron Gray is driving and his father Cyril is on the back.

> There were ten children in the end. My grandparents slept in the middle room upstairs with the boys on one side and the girls on the other. Father had to take the milk to Tisbury in a horse and cart. It was always bad at Chicksgrove where the water could be right up to the shafts whenever there was heavy rain. Sometimes we had as many as ten Guernsey

cows and an allotment opposite – everyone in Sutton Row had an allotment.

When Ron's father, Cyril, returned from the First World War, he supplemented the family income by working as the village carrier. He purchased what was presumed to be the first bus in the area, an old Ford model T, which he housed in a lean-to garage erected against the barn. He brought back orders from Salisbury and carried passengers. On the way home they had to get out and walk the steep ascent of Jay's Folly!

Ron went to the village school but at the age of eleven most pupils transferred to the larger school at neighbouring Fovant. Bicycles were provided for their journey. His final years there, however, showed a declining attendance:

I left school at fourteen to help father but in the last year I was home more than at school else I would have got a good hiding! From an early age I was drawing water from the well in a 5-gallon bucket to drag up the road for the stock. Then there was the milking, mucking out, hedging with a hook, haymaking, harrowing and rolling. There was plenty to do whatever the season.

We had a double piggery here and a bacon rack in the living room. We fed the pigs on scraps and killed them at October time when the flies were gone. We salted them and they would last the year round. It was beautiful bacon. You could enjoy it with cider made from the trees here, now long gone. The old ones were always calling for a drink and a chat in those days.

During the Second World War, I worked at Manor Farm. At that time all the downs were ploughed to get more corn. That's why I didn't go in the army, there was about 500 acres to work. Dad had to work on his own. Then he bought 50 acres of corn and I came home to help him. When times got bad and my son wasn't interested in carrying on the farm I sold most of it.

By the turn of the 20th century, Ron Gray had only 6 acres left to work. The barn, now topped with galvanised iron instead of thatch, is filled with the ageing agricultural relics of his trade. The cow byres, and the outside shed with two coppers – one to boil the pig food and the other for the washing – remain each side of the defunct bread oven, all overlaid with dust. The little hut where Granfer Gray mended shoes for the villagers retains its tools and rusting nails.

Dorothy Mullins with her father Frank outside the Glasses Lane cottage. Between them is Dorothy's neice, four-year-old Margaret Mullins, who continued to live there until her death in 2004. Gilbert Mullins, one of Frank's thirteen sons, is to their right.

Margaret Mullins lived until the end of her life in a picturesque cottage on Glasses Hill south of the village, on a steep, winding lane to the A30. In 1881 her grandparents, Frank and Margaret Mullins, were living at Slate Cottage, neighbours of the Grays in Sutton Row. Here they raised their family of thirteen boys followed by one daughter, Dorothy, who remained unmarried, devoting her life to this large family. Later they moved to Ivy Cottage opposite the Old Rectory. Here Frank, described in Kelly's Directory as 'a cottage farmer', had a smallholding and pasturage for his cow. In 1917 he bought the Glasses Hill cottage when the sale of the Wyndham property released it. This was the only home Margaret had known.

Frank Mullins and his large family are long dead now but most left their mark on the village: Alfred kept the village shop – mainly sweets and tobacco – in a cottage at

Sutton

The Mullins family at Farm Orchard, Sutton Mandeville, early 20th century. Frank and Margaret (mother and father) are surrounded by eleven of their thirteen sons, with their only daughter, Dorothy, behind them. The sons are (left to right), back row: Sid, Alf, Fred, Ed, Walt, Gil, William; front row: Harry, Frank, Thomas, James. John and Mark are not present.

Sutton Cross; Harry worked on the land; Walt became landlord of the Cross Keys Inn at Fovant; Gil was a local gardener; Jim, the youngest, is named on the memorial tablet in the church – killed in action in the First World War; Fred, too, died young, killed in Sutton Street when his horse and cart bolted; Tom, the eldest, was a local carpenter, Sidney, Margaret's father, survived the longest, dying in 1974 aged ninety.

Margaret, too, spent her life in the local community:

I went to the old school here with Freddie Spenser and Ron Gray. There was about twenty-five to thirty pupils and two teachers. At fourteen I left school to become a parlour maid at Brookside. This was a large house at Fovant belonging to Captain and Mrs Norman. Mrs Norman was very strict and when we went to a dance we had to return by ten and knock her bedroom door when we got back! After three years they moved to London and I was employed by the Ridouts at the farmhouse near Fovant Church. At Brookside there had been a cook and housemaid as well as me. At the Ridouts I had to do everything!'

During the war, Margaret left to work at RAF Chilmark. Here she worked for thirty-three years, starting with munitions' inspection and finishing at the Officers' Mess. After retirement, she continued to live in the Glasses Hill cottage tending her garden and surrounded by the memorabilia of her large family, until her death in 2004.

Sutton Mandeville school group, 1934. Included in the line-up are Margaret Mullins (back row, first girl from left), Ron Gray (in front of Margaret), and Fred Spenser, the miller's grandson (standing, third boy from left)

15

Fovant

the Fading Downland
Badges

ANYONE TRAVELLING along the beautiful stretch of the A30 between Wilton and Shaftesbury will have noted its most dramatic feature – the Fovant Badges. They were cut into the chalk downland by First World War troops and form the largest group of hill figures in Europe. It is sad to think that this startling tribute to those who served in two world wars could itself be suffering a period of terminal decline. Already much of the finer detail has disappeared, but an energetic committee of the Fovant Badges Society is working hard to preserve at least some of them.

Fovant High Street in 1919, showing Mrs Truckel's sweet and grocery shop to the right.

Fovant lies at right angles to the open downland, its stream running from a spring-fed lake, beneath the A30 and through the village, to meet the Nadder at Dinton. Overbuilding is restricted by the contours of the valley but an attractive blend of old and modern buildings lies along its busy main street.

Fovant was fortunate in having Richard Clay as its historian and doctor. Born in 1890, he was the third

Fovant Church, early 20th century

generation of the practice started there by his grandfather in 1855. Described by many who knew him as 'one of the best types of country doctor', he served both Fovant and the surrounding area until just before his death in 1971, aged eighty. He was also an antiquarian of repute whose excavation of the downland between the Ebble and Nadder Valleys has yielded valuable knowledge of the Iron Age period.

Clay described the prehistoric valley of Fovant as an undrained swamp with tangled trees and thick undergrowth. Although numerous flint implements indicate early lowland settlements, it was not until the Iron Age that the hill fortress of Chiselbury Ring provided protection for farming communities on the downland. By Roman times, however, all habitation had disappeared. After AD 552, following the Battle of Old Sarum, Saxon tribesmen founded *Fobbanfunta* (the 'fountain' or 'stream' of Fobba). This was the original settlement of Fovant which at that time included Sutton Mandeville. Saxon charters confirm that by the 10th century it had become the possession of the abbey at Wilton.

The 15th-century church at Fovant hides down a short lane north of the village but is worth visiting for its elaborately carved tower, battlemented and with fierce-looking gargoyles. There is an interesting brass in the chancel, wisely covered with perspex, commemorating the building of this tower by the rector, George Rede. He is shown with his rosary beside the Virgin Mary at the Annunciation with the angel at her feet.

The patron of the living was from early times the abbey of Wilton, one of the richest in England. Cicely Bodenham was installed as abbess by Henry VIII in 1535. It was an unorthodox appointment as she had never been a nun at the convent, but was supposedly more compliant to the transfer of power to the Crown. When the abbey was finally surrendered in 1539 she was allowed, against normal tradition, to remain in the area, taking for her residence the manor house adjacent to Fovant Church. Thirty-one of her nuns found refuge in more modest local accommodation.

The old Salisbury to Shaftesbury road, the Upper Herepath, has previously been mentioned. It had carried the main route from early times along the downland ridge and was described in 1448 as 'the best road from London to the West'. At that time it was used mainly by teams of pack horses with the occasional cumbersome post wagons drawn by teams of horses. In 1658 increasing traffic included the first post coach travelling at 3 miles per hour. With remote parishes responsible for maintenance, the road surface soon deteriorated; numerous complaints were made concerning its appalling condition.

Not surprisingly for such an isolated stretch of road, highwaymen abounded – despite the ominous presence of the Gallows Tree a few miles west of Fovant Hut. Cunning Dick was one such character whose favourite site for hold-ups was a ridge of downs between Fovant Hut and Chiselbury Camp.

Improvements in maintenance and security came in 1761 when the old road became a turnpike. Nevertheless, problems remained, not least with the steep descent at White Sheet Hill. A petition to Parliament in 1768 requested the Lower Way from Donhead to Barford be used as a turnpike which 'will not only prove very advantageous to the inhabitants, but much more convenient to the Public, as being nearer than any other road, and having no Hills to prevent expedition'. The petition was successful and by 1792 the new turnpike was legalised. The Fovant Turnpike Gate was situated at the border with Compton Chamberlayne.

Like the other south bank villages of the Nadder, Fovant was to benefit from the development of the new London to Exeter road now known as the A30. In December 1792 the *Salisbury Journal* announced the opening of a new inn with stabling for twenty horses opposite the 17th-century Cross Keys Inn:

right] A road maintenance gang at Fovant in the early 1930s, while carrying out general improvements to the B3089 road at Dinton. Fred Mullins is the roadman second from left.

below] Walter and Florence Mullins on their wedding day outside the Cross Keys Inn, Fovant. They took over running the inn in the late 1920s following the death of Florence's parents, Elizabeth and Edwin Perrett.

NEW ROAD from Salisbury to Shaftesbury – James Millard begs Leave to inform Ladies and Gentlemen, and Travellers in general, that he has taken and fitted up that large and commodious new-built Inn, the Pembroke Arms, at Fovant, where he flatters himself that he shall merit their favours and support, as he has laid in an assortment of good old Wines and other Liquors. Good beds, well aired. Neat Post Chaises, with able Horses, and careful Drivers.

The postboy of a coach always sounded his horn when approaching Fovant. A bell was then rung at the inn to summon the ostlers to change the horses.

By 1850 local traffic included one mail coach each way daily between London and the west travelling at 13 miles per hour. Four years later a report to Parliament once more complained 'of the dangerous and disgraceful condition of the turnpike under Salisbury Plain'. Within a few years, however, the new railway line was built through Dinton and the

coach traffic diminished. The last coach driver from
Shaftesbury was reputedly Henry Coombes who was noted
for the redness of his face and the watery appearance of his
eyes, peculiarities he attributed to the action of wind and
rain rather than the large amount of liquid which went
down his throat! In 1889 the new county council took
responsibility for all main roads. Since then the creation of
the First World War army camps and the increasing
demands of modern traffic have led to successive
improvements and road-widening schemes along the A30.

With the outbreak of war in August 1914, Fovant was
transformed as the need to find training accommodation for
British, and later Commonwealth, troops became
paramount. Much good agricultural land was taken over for
a network of huts spreading from Sutton Mandeville to

Fovant garrison cinema.
Performances were held twice
nightly for the troops.
Admission was 3d and 6d or
1s if a seat was reserved.

National Stores, Fovant during the 1st World War. The proprietor was John White, a grocer from Wilton.

Sgt Drummer Richard Cooper of the Notts & Derby Regiment being presented with the DCM outside the Cross Keys Inn, one of a number of decorations being presented by King George V for gallantry in Ireland, 12 February 1917

Barford St Martin. A bustling military township soon developed with parade grounds, rifle ranges, a military hospital and all the paraphernalia of war. A wide range of shops, tea rooms and service facilities rapidly evolved. There was even a garrison cinema showing twice nightly the current releases of Chaplin, Keaton and other popular screen heroes of the day.

In late 1915 Edwin Rixon, the Chilmark stonemason, was one of those helping to construct a branch line from Dinton replacing much less efficient transportation by mules. Troop trains and goods trains rumbled through continuously and convoys of wounded soldiers travelled from the south-coast ports to the large military hospital close to the Fovant railhead. It was by car, however, that George V travelled from Dinton station in February 1917.

He presented decorations outside the Pembroke Arms and inspected the troops before observing a demonstration of bombing at trenches on West Farm.

Within this imposed township, many thousands of men from regular and territorial units as well as Australians carried out their training before going into action. As troops, with their horses and gun carriages, passed through the villages an initial reaction of misgiving soon gave way to a patriotic acceptance. Thousands of soldiers were welcomed into local homes. Miss Constance Penruddocke, for example, from her home in Dinton entertained numerous Australian soldiers and wrote letters home for them. Her correspondence is now in the Hall of Memory in Canberra.

At the conclusion of the war, the camp became one of the largest demobilisation centres in the country. One of the Langdon family from Compton Chamberlayne was demobilised from here. When offered his rail warrant to go

Outside Albert Jukes's shop in Fovant at the beginning of the 20th century. Note the un-made condition of the road. A trade directory of 1907 suggests that he also ran the stores in Compton Chamberlayne.

Tom Coombes of Fovant among the war graves in the churchyard, 1920

home, he replied that he only had a five-minute walk to get there! It was not until 1920 that the last of the troops departed leaving behind a tangled web of hut foundations and concrete roads for the unfortunate farmers to remove before their land could be restored. Military graves, many of Australian service men who died of injuries or the infamous 1918-19 'flu epidemic, can be seen in churchyards at Fovant, Compton Chamberlayne, Barford and Baverstock. A more prominent reminder of those times is, of course, the badges.

The idea of cutting regimental badges into the downland originated in 1916 with the London Rifle Brigade. Theirs was the smallest, but by the end of the war a wide range of emblems, some as big as a football pitch, gave an indication of the units situated in the district. There was no lack of volunteers even though the work had to be done on steep slopes and between 4 am and 7 am, before the firing parties arrived on the ranges. Laurence Combes, in his compilation *Badges in the Chalk,* gives a fair indication of the work that had to be done:

> The first job was to mark out the badges to scale, in itself no mean task. Then followed the removal of the turf, after which the cavities had to be filled with chalk dug from nearby pits, for the natural chalk lies too far below the surface to be exposed by the mere removal of turf. Sergeant F. Hall, of the 6th City of London Rifles, who was in charge of the working party on his badge, stated that it took three months to complete which gives some idea of the magnitude of the task, the overall height of that badge being 150 ft. At the end of each early morning's work, the men would toboggan down the grassy slope on their shovels to receive a well-earned breakfast.

Recent defence cuts have considerably worsened the problems of renovation resulting in reduced funding and fewer working parties. Roy Nuttall, previous secretary of the Fovant Badges Society which has organised restoration over many years, was convinced that the badges would disappear by the end of the 20th century unless national assistance was forthcoming. A new committee took positive steps to ensure this did not happen, but, sadly, some badges will be left to fade away in the chalk downland. At the society's headquarters in

An aerial view of Fovant badges below the Iron Age fortress of Chiselbury Camp. Behind can be seen the line of the old Salisbury to Shaftesbury road, a main route to the west before the A30 was developed from 1792

Charles Mason, carpenter, at work on the coffer and screen for Fovant church. The wood was cut from Hyde's Copse, Dinton

the Pembroke Arms, a wide range of First World War memorabilia can be seen. Amongst them is a poem by an anonymous soldier which concludes:

> It is some relief to get a job, 'volunteers to muster'
> To climb the hill, and dig, an addition to the cluster
> Of Regimental badges which we uphold with pride
> And leave behind a memory upon the green hillside

It will be a cause of national regret if the Nadder Valley loses such a treasured symbol of the ordinary people, urban and rural, who dwelt among them at that time.

16

Compton Chamberlayne the Rising in the West

William and Emily Langdon of Manor Farm, Compton Chamberlayne before the 1st World War

A S YOU ENTER Compton Chamberlayne from the A30 you will see the plum coloured walls of Martins Meadow. It is the home of Willie Langdon and his wife and was converted by them from two farm cottages when they retired from Naish's Farm. In it, they will show you a table constructed from an elm tree that blew down in a storm during the 1890s. The elm had been planted in the grounds of Compton Park to commemorate the restoration of Charles II. It symbolised the long association of the village with the Royalist cause and the public execution of one of its noblest residents.

The village itself, with a population of ninety-two, has changed very little, possibly less than any other in the

Nadder Valley. It displays with pride the 'Best Kept Small Village in Wiltshire' sign, won on a number of occasions. Its single street is lined with a rich variety of local-stone cottages of all shapes and sizes, buildings of character, many with a story of their own: The Admiral's House, The Old School House, The Dower House and Kings Elm, once the village pub. Camel Cottage derives its name from its unusually humped, thatched roof. Piggots, the oldest residence, is named after one of its owners, reputedly the last survivor of the infamous Black Hole of Calcutta. His tombstone can be found near the church path.

The briefest reference in Domesday indicates that the original name of the village was Contone, 'a village in the valley'. The name changed during the medieval period when

Compton Chamberlayne House. Built originally in Tudor Gothic style in 1550 by Sir Edward Penruddocke, it was later remodelled in the early Stuart style and remained with the family until 1930.

ownership of the estate fell to Robert le Chamberlayne. At that time the manor comprised two woods, a mill, pasture and meadow, a total of 2,000 acres. Compton House is set among sweeping parkland, with the elegant lake added much later. It was originally built in Tudor Gothic style in 1550, the creation of Sir Edward Penruddocke whose family came from the Cumberland village of Penruddocke on the slopes of Skiddaw. It was later remodelled in the early Stuart style with beautiful dining room carvings from the workshops of Grinling Gibbons. The estate was to remain with the family for nearly four centuries.

A record of the Penruddockes from 1598 to 1924 can be seen on the north wall of the chancel of St Michael's Church. Below it, the chancel floor has been raised to accommodate their many tombs. Chief among its sons was Sir John Penruddocke who had lost a brother in the Civil War but continued to work unsparingly in his efforts to set Charles II on the throne. Following the Battle of Worcester he led the Rising in the West, part of a poorly orchestrated and unsuccessful national revolt against Cromwell.

It was early in the morning of 12 March 1655 when Colonel Sir John Penruddocke, accompanied by other prominent Royalist leaders, marched into Salisbury with two hundred men, hoping to gain further aid. They quickly gained possession of the prison where willing supporters were found, but when Charles II was proclaimed in the market-place, the townspeople, no doubt aware of Cromwell's military strength, remained unenthusiastic. Two circuit judges and the high sheriff, Colonel John Dove, were forced from their beds. The judges were later released but the sheriff, still clad in night attire, was taken hostage.

Penruddocke and his associates galloped westwards, hoping to reach their Cornish allies with an army of men recruited on the way. The response was disappointing. Cromwell, well briefed on the plot from the beginning, commissioned his brother-in-law John Desborough to unite the Puritan units of the west against them. Captain Unton Croke, however, Commander of Exeter's single troop of regimental cavalry, was in a better position to intercede. He caught up with the Royalists at South Molton. Tired, dispirited and sapped by desertions, the rebels gave little resistance. Many fled and the remainder, including John Penruddocke, were taken as prisoners to Exeter.

Throughout his period of imprisonment and trial, John Penruddocke was loyally supported by his wife, Arundel. Left with seven children, she petitioned continually for his reprieve. It was to no avail. Their correspondence, reflecting mutual devotion, is very moving. On the day the death warrant was announced, and she knew her efforts to have been in vain, Arundel penned one final letter, surely among the loveliest and most moving of billet-doux:

> My dear heart,
> My sad parting was so far from making me to forget you, that I have scarce thought upon myself since, but wholly upon you. Those dear embraces which I yet feel, and shall never lose (being the faithful testimonies of an indulgent husband) have charmed my soul to such a reverence of your remembrances, that were it possible, I would with my own blood cement your dead limbs to life again, and with reverence think it no sin to rob heaven a little longer of a martyr . . .

right] Village scene in Compton Chamberlayne, early 1900s. The provisions shop on the left remained open until recent times.

With his co-conspirator, Colonel Hugh Grove, John Penruddocke was beheaded, having faced his execution with dignity and courage.

Apparently the loyalty shown to the Stuarts continued into the next century, for a Charles Penruddocke in the time of the Pretenders refused to attend the Georgian court. A portrait of him at Compton Park showed him in plain hunting attire instead of the court dress of other family members. Tradition maintains that he joined with other

like-minded gentlemen of the neighbourhood at the Cribbage Hut at nearby Sutton Mandeville. Here, under the pretext of playing cribbage, the Stuart interests were discussed and toasts drunk to 'The King Over the Water!'

The feudal grip of the Penruddockes at Compton Chamberlayne remained until well into the last century. The squire's high-handed attitude to the newly created parish council is illustrated in the Minute Book for 1897. Councillors protested about Charles Penruddocke taking the chair when seeking re-election for the post. Six months later they objected to the parish meetings being held within the hall of Compton House. This paternalistic attitude within the village, often benignly expressed, is reflected in the memoirs of a life-long resident, Mrs Hilda Kerley:

The church, St Michael's, was warm and comfortable, heated by a large stove in the middle. The organ was played by Mr Fry, with members of his family around him leading the singing. Squire and his family always sat in the chancel, tenant farmers to the right of the church and to the left it was for the Park servants and employees.

right] Army Camp No 11 at Compton Chamberlayne during winter. This was one of twelve 1st World War camps in the parish. Visible on the hillside behind the huts is the map of Australia carved in the chalk.

The vicar was Mr Dudley Digges. He was getting on in years then, but he was a good preacher and the parishioners were his interest and care. Each Christmas one shilling for each household he paid into the shop so that they could have something extra for their tea on Christmas Day.

At that time, Compton Chamberlayne represented the classical integration of manor house, park, church and village supported entirely by an agricultural economy. The three large farms and several smallholdings provided work for the labourers and were well supported by a variety of estate craftsmen. In addition, a well-run market garden had developed. There was an active forge and a spar and hurdle maker, John Wyatt. The post office and stores sold everything from paraffin and coal to a packet of pins. Clement Barnes had shown a surprising business acumen by converting Compton Hut on the downs into 'apartments for down air 620 ft above sea level' (later to become a home for consumptives). But this was 1913. The village was on the verge of great change:

Then came the war and village life changed almost overnight. Some of the young men were territorials and were soon called up. Then it was decided on building camps here, and all we could hear were huge traction engines along the main road, tearing it up with their heavy loads of timber and thousands of workmen from all parts of Britain descended on the countryside, till it was like one big city stretching from Barford St Martin to Fovant.

Life in the village varied now from day to day. Men worked harder in the fields, and women in the little leisure time they had were knitting socks and making shirts. When the

Running the flag in 1951 on the map of Australia carved on Compton Down by Australian troops during the 1st World War

troops arrived at the camps around, the place was altered altogether. They swarmed everywhere and the London regiments ruined everything by tearing up flowers and sending them back home. For some it was their first time in the countryside. They were fond of calling our village 'Compton Chamberlayne-in-the-Mud'.

Following the Armistice, life in the village changed again. The troops eventually left and the farm labourers gradually returned. But the leisurely, close-knit texture of the community was beginning to break down. 'Most of the old people were gone, bewailed Mrs Kerley, 'and those who were here were more restless.' The reasons for this change were complex and reflected the decline in rural living all over the country. The First World War had given its younger generation glimpses of a wider world. The development of the internal combustion engine had its effects, with Mr Jarvis's bus from Fovant there was no more walking three miles to Dinton station in order to get to Salisbury. Finally, the brief prosperity of the immediate postwar years gave way to slump with the 'drift from the land' gathering momentum as agricultural wages fell dramatically and the workers were forced to look to the towns.

Depression struck at the very heart of Compton Chamberlayne. After four centuries, the Penruddocke occupancy finally came to an end in 1930. The old squire, Charles Penruddocke, saddened by the loss of two of his sons in the war and impoverished by falling land values, had died in the previous year. Edward Rixon, the stonemason, attended the sale of Compton Park from his new home at Barford, finding 'things rather dear, a grand house but got in very poor condition'. Apart from Manor Farm the entire estate passed to George Cross, a London businessman-cum-farmer. Through the mid-century, the village was transformed as farms became increasingly mechanised. With less and less labour required, the cottages fell into private hands.

Today only the Langdons and the Lovells remain of the 'old' community. Willie Langdon, grandson of the William Langdon who worked Manor Farm from 1895 to 1920, returned to the village in 1943 to work Naish's Farm until his retirement. Valentine Lovell came to the village in 1915 as landlord of the King's Elm, a beer and cider house – there was never a licence for spirits. In 1929 he took over

Charles Penruddocke, the last of the family to be lords of the manor of Compton Chamberlayne over four centuries. He died in 1929 and the house and land were sold.

Home Farm with his two sons and farmed it until his death in 1988 when it was taken back into the estate. Today his grandson Richard works part time on the estate. He is also building up a successful pigeon-shooting business for clients all over the world. Perhaps this is the kind of flexibility we should be looking for to keep our villages alive.

17
Burcombe
a Misplaced Village

URCOMBE MAY WELL BE UNIQUE in that part of its area was omitted from earlier maps by an oversight. When preparing his map of Wiltshire, John Speed, who died in 1629, copied the work of a previous cartographer and surveyor, Christopher Saxton. He noticed that Saxton showed a village between Barford St Martin and Ugford that was not named. He wrote the word *Quare* (presumably 'query') against it, intending to check it later. This he failed to do and the word was engraved and printed on his map. Later cartographers copied Speed's work and the famous Quare maps of Wiltshire appeared until the mistake was rectified 145 years later.

left] A tea break during threshing on the downs above Burcombe. The team travelled from farm to farm. One of this team was later burnt to death when his caravan caught fire during the night.

The missing village was North Burcombe where today little more than the redundant church of St John the Baptist remains of a once-flourishing community. The church, too, is unusual in that its tower is lower than the roof of the nave. It may claim to be among the oldest in the Nadder Valley for it is of Saxon origin. Chandler and Parker, in their recently-revised book *The Church in Wiltshire,* warn against identifying churches as having been built at a particular period. Usually the original building underwent drastic change. Constant additions and modifications were made throughout the Middle Ages as repairs and the needs of the community dictated. But at Burcombe there is clear evidence of the survival of a Saxon chancel with its distinctive long-and-short work on the corners of the external masonry.

The church was most inconveniently placed for the existing village. South Burcombe, now known simply as Burcombe, lies in the valley across the busy A30. From the graveyard

left] Church of St John the Baptist, Burcombe, early last century. Unusually, the tower of the church is lower than the nave. There is clear evidence of the survival of a Saxon chancel here, with its distinctive long-and-short work on the corners of the external masonry.

one has a magnificent view of the flood plain of the Nadder below and the multi-arched bridge which takes you to the village centre. Beyond lies the chalk downland where ancient trackways lead 600 ft up to the Punch Bowl just below the ridge. Here, numerous earthworks remain, memorials to Neolithic and Bronze Age tribes who were the first to inhabit the area. Later the Saxon incursors called their valley settlement Brydancumb, or Bryda's Valley, but traditions of a separate church of St Peter there are unlikely to be true. South Burcombe was a vast boggy area when the Abbesses of Wilton allowed St John's to be built on the higher ground.

There is, however, evidence of the deserted village of South Ugford in fields below the present hamlet. This was believed to contain a chapel of its own. Surprisingly, until 1882, Burcombe stretched well beyond Ugford to include a portion of Wilton as far as the Bell Inn and the Priory and Hospice of St John. Originally the church at Burcombe had been a mere chapel-of-ease belonging to this priory, and a strong association continued between them.

In 1859 the first of several Victorian restorations to the Burcombe church took place. On this occasion, under the supervision of the cathedral architect T H Wyatt, the whole building was reroofed, refloored and the old pews replaced. Usually one hears little of the ceremony and jollifications that accompanied these occasions but a letter from the vicar, Rev. Edward Trotman, many years later gives an interesting picture of the celebrations here:

Never shall I forget the re-opening on September 27th, 1859. The procession of parishioners wending its way across the bridge from the village headed by the brass band which Burcombe then possessed, was witnessed by a company of visitors from the Parsonage garden. It was a very pretty sight. The saintly Bishop Hamilton officiated at the morning service, with the Rev C B Pearson, then Prior of St John's Hospital. Few indeed are now surviving who can remember the dinner under the elm trees which followed the morning service.

One little incident I must record. A few days before the opening, Mr Sidney Herbert had a shooting party. He most kindly sent 'the bag', which was on wheels, to me for the proposed entertainment of my friends and parishioners: it consisted of 60 brace of partridges and 13 hares. I had other presents of the same kind from Hurdcote, Compton and Dinton, with the result that on the plate of every adult resident in Burcombe, was a cold roast partridge. The children had tea on the lawn. There was a second service late in the afternoon, at which the Prior Pearson preached. I can truly say that never was a church restoration more needed, more appreciated at the time, and followed by a more distinct improvement in church feeling and church conduct.

Burcombe had now reached its population peak, four hundred and twenty in the 1851 Census, (including part of Wilton), and was in the process of assuming the pattern we see today. It was still the small farming community it had always been but this was a period of great improvement to farm houses, cottages and farm buildings on the Pembroke estates. At Burcombe new buildings gradually blended with the old. The 17th-century farmhouse was soon to be joined by the more elegant manor. Nearby, in short rows, were the labourers' cottages all in the distinctive Pembroke style: chalk-stone walls with high, pointed gables and slate roofs. Further west lay the mill, mentioned in Domesday. Above the mill stream was the Ship Inn where, in 1867, John Hibberd served the dual role of shopkeeper and publican. Opposite lay one of the few 15th-century cruck-built hall houses still existing in the Nadder Valley. Known as Juniper Cottage, this served for a while as the village post office. In 1876, where the roads meet, a school, now the village hall, was built. This replaced a small thatched room which then became a reading-room for the recreation of the estate workers.

Burcombe

right] The Ship at Burcombe during the 1st World War, with Australian soldiers standing in front. The cottage in the centre was later demolished.

below] Ben and Jane Gumbleton, publicans from the Ship Inn, with their son Alfred and Jane's sister, early 1920s. Ben was an ex-Coldstream Guardsman and 6ft 4ins tall.

By the beginning of the last century the population had fallen dramatically as the effects of agricultural depression and the demolition of older, more dilapidated cottages took their toll. When Benjamin and Jane Gumbleton arrived at the Ship in 1912 they found a community much affected by the fall in land values. Their daughter, Violet Cheverall, was born there in 1922 and remembered the hardships of those days:

My parents came from the Winchester area where they had been involved with two pubs. The only trade we had at the Ship was with the villagers – apart from a party of bookies who came down occasionally from the Salisbury Races and enjoyed enormous meals. The kiddies used to scramble for their change. The Slate Club had their big occasion at Christmas. As people had so little money, most customers' debts were 'slated' until the end of the week or, in many cases, until Michaelmas. Many farm workers brought their bread and cheese with an onion up at night and father had a big bowl of lentil soup always ready in the winter. Tommy Churchill used to give me a piece of stale dough cake which I ate on his step opposite the mill.

There was one poor old lady, Mrs Vine, who was over ninety when she died. She wore a man's hat over hair plastered with vaseline and arrived at the pub each morning with her toby jug and old clay pipe. She would fill her jug and put all the old fag ends into her pipe. My father was always sympathetic to her and kept her jug filled from the slops dripping from the tap. There was a pet duck, too, who got drunk regularly on those drippings!

Another interesting custom of this era is mentioned in the Barford and Burcombe WI Scrapbook. Newspapers were not delivered to the village as they are today. Only a few people had them. These few papers were thrown each day from the train. At Barford St Martin this was at the Dairy

A charabanc outing, 1926, from Burcombe – probably to Weymouth or Bournemouth. The Sparrow & Vincent bus is from Salisbury. Vi Cheverell and her mother Jane, from the Ship Inn, are in the centre. Vi recalled that the children were always given a bag of gooseberries, and a streamer to throw from the bus.

Road bridge, known then as 'One-eyed Arch', where whoever happened to be around picked them up and placed them on 'The Paper Stone' near the rectory. At Burcombe, Jack, a small dog, would wait for the paper train to come through. When they were thrown from the train he would pick them up in his teeth and drag them to the adjacent vicarage. His grave is by the side of the railway line where he used to wait, just inside the vicarage garden.

Burcombe school photograph, c. 1918. Violet Cheverell's brother, Alfred Gumbleton, is seated far right. He later worked as a telegraph boy at Wilton but died aged 17.

In 1930 George Waters resided at the manor still farming 'in the old fashioned way – with carters and cowmen, shepherds and a drowner for the water meadows'. He had a steam engine and threshers; his labourers did the thatching. He used hurdles for his Hampshire Down sheep and milked by hand in sheds. By 1935 Sidney Pond, the new tenant farmer, realised that survival in agriculture called for a more pragmatic approach. He cut his work force from twenty-four to eight, got rid of the sheep and concentrated on dairy farming introducing mechanical milking in the open air.

A G Street, in his book *Farmer's Glory*, wrote graphically of the difficulties of introducing the new milking methods when trying to save nearby Ditchampton Farm from bankruptcy. Not surprisingly, it was the cows that caused most of the problems:

> We started at 4 am as we needed to start milking at 5 am, and we had anticipated a little difficulty in getting the herd into the enclosure. A little difficulty! Ye gods! The labours of Hercules must have been child's play compared to it.
>
> There were about six of us, including a man sent to instruct us by the makers of the outfit. We found the herd and proceeded to drive them towards the enclosure. They went quietly enough until they got quite near to the outfit, and then they stampeded in all directions.
>
> If there was one corner of that pasture to which those cows were not going, it was the one which was occupied by the outfit. 'Anywhere but there' was their motto. Why should respectable, aged ladies be subjected to these new indignities? Where were their old comfortable buildings in which each one had her particular stall by right of long tenancy? And who were these fools who persisted in attempting to drive them away from their old home?

Despite Sidney Pond's innovations, he continued to live the life of a country squire residing in the manor

right] Burcombe Manor, built in the mid-19th century, reputedly to house Lord Herbert of Lea, the friend and supporter of Florence Nightingale.

described rather grandly as 'a Mansion House with Gardens, Pleasure Grounds and Office'. The estate was kept immaculately. Every other year all the men took two weeks to cut the beautiful yew hedge surrounding the manor. After his death in 1965, the new tenants, Mick and Sue Combes, were forced to consider a more cost-effective lifestyle. They moved from the manor to the adjoining dairy house. This they converted into an attractive farmhouse, providing bed and breakfast as a sideline. Today, the sheep are back on the Burcombe fields and Mick farms 860 acres with his son, Nicholas, and the latest in agricultural technology.

18

Wilton

Ancient Capital of Wessex

I T IS FITTING that the River Nadder should finish its individual existence at Wilton, the jewel in its crown. Here, it meets its picturesque neighbour, the Wylye, just east of the town. Together they join the Avon at Salisbury, to begin the final journey to Christchurch and the sea.

Because of its low-lying position, the Celts and Romans showed little interest in this confluence of rivers, preferring to develop their roads on higher ground – the tracks through Grovely and the southern ridge referred to so often. It was the marauding Saxons, seeking to expand their influence from their tribal base at Old Sarum, who found in Wilton a far more accessible and well-watered site. It possessed rich agricultural land and its position between the two rivers and the downland ridgeways made it easy to protect.

By AD 800, Wilton had become a royal town, with Egbert having a palace traditionally believed to be in Kingsbury Square. At that time the town would have centred on Four Corners – the area where the roads cross at the traffic lights. Here was space for the development of a market-place with its surrounding buildings as well as the church of St Mary.

It may well have been from Wilton that Egbert's grandson, Alfred, planned his many skirmishes against the Danes. During his reign it achieved acclaim as the one of the capitals of Wessex, an area stretching across the southern region of England. Although he later moved his capital to Winchester, Wilton remained a key defensive location and an administrative centre of a region that grew into the county of Wiltshire. The growth of its influence and wealth during the early Middle Ages was partly due to its abbey, one of the

The famous sheep fair at Wilton which has taken place over centuries. This view of the fairground to the north of the town dates from the early 20th century.

great religious foundations of England. Although its origin is obscure the abbey was certainly in existence by 934 as in that year King Athelstan granted it land.

The moving story of Wilton's patron saint, Edith, is first related in a 15th-century poem in Wiltshire dialect. The young King Edgar stayed at the abbey around 959 and was strongly attracted to Wulfrith, a young nun of good birth. The king's desires could not be ignored and after becoming pregnant Wulfrith retreated to Kent where their daughter, Edith, was born. Wulfrith later returned to the abbey and became its abbess, bringing with her Edith, who was by now a young woman noted for her pious living. Despite offers of high office, Edith preferred to remain at Wilton devoting herself to good works. Her early death was said to be a cause of great sorrow not just in Wilton but throughout the country. Pilgrims to her shrine during later centuries contributed to the fame and prosperity enjoyed by the abbey.

During these early years of its existence, Wilton suffered many setbacks including the devastation caused by the Danish invasion of 1003 which burnt it to the ground. Despite such disasters, by the 12th century it had developed into a successful industrial centre. As an important market between east and west its many crafts flourished. The existence of a royal mint until the 13th century is further evidence of its importance.

Of the numerous churches that existed in medieval times – no fewer than twelve – only the priory of St John and the ruins of the old parish church of St Mary in the

The Six Bells in North Street, Wilton. A very old public house which belonged to Folliott's brewery, now defunct, whose premises occupied the corner of Rollestone Street and Winchester Street in Salisbury.

market-place remain today. When Bishop Poore decided to remove the Norman cathedral from its inhospitable site on Old Sarum, it was to Wilton that he first turned to build the new one. It is interesting to speculate that, had the abbess not refused his request, the future of Wilton might have been considerably different. Later, when Bishop Bingham was consecrated, the ceremony was performed at St Mary's Church, Wilton, as the new cathedral was not yet ready. This provides another ironic twist to Wilton's fortunes as it was he who decided to build a bridge at Harnham thus diverting the town's lucrative markets to Salisbury. Inevitably its trade declined, but Wilton retained its borough status through the charter granted by Henry I in 1100, the oldest existing charter document in the country.

With the dissolution of its famous abbey in 1539, Wilton began a new era. The estate was given to William Herbert who was married to the sister of Henry VIII's last wife,

Catherine Parr. Later to become the first Earl of Pembroke, he cleared most of the abbey site to build his new home, a residence planned by the court painter, Holbein. During the Elizabethan era this was to bring Wilton into prominence with a golden age of its own. The countess, Mary, wife of the second earl, was sister to Sir Philip Sidney who was one of the great cultural figures of the day. At Wilton he wrote much of his greatest masterpiece, *Arcadia*. Lady Mary, too, was an accomplished person and through her influence many of the notable literary figures of the time made their way to Wilton. Shakespeare, the greatest of them all, is believed to have performed *As You Like It* there for the first time in the presence of King James I.

In 1648 a disastrous fire all but destroyed the Elizabethan mansion. The house was replaced by the fourth earl, using Inigo Jones and his nephew, John Webb, as his chief architects. A handsome Palladian bridge, added later in 1737, can also be seen in the pleasure gardens as it crosses the Nadder. So much has been written about this beautiful house and its treasures, visited yearly by thousands of tourists, that it would be superfluous to say more. As principal landowners, employers and patrons, however, the Pembrokes have continued to influence Wilton and its surrounding area to the present day. Particularly important to the town was their help in creating a new carpet industry at a time when the old weaving industry was declining.

The Wilton Royal Carpet Factory, reputedly the oldest in the world, traces its origin to a charter by William III in 1699 to establish the 'mystery and fellowship' of weaving. There is a persistent legend that it was started by two Huguenot weavers fleeing from religious persecution on the continent. Although forbidden to leave, an amusing tradition has it that they were smuggled into England in empty wine barrels by the Lord Pembroke of the day, and that with his encouragement they set up looms and produced carpets by a unique process which became known as the Wilton Weave. The business flourished to the extent that both Wilton and, later, Axminster carpets were exported all over the world.

The cynical closure of the Wilton Royal Carpet Factory in 1995 by an American multinational company caused outrage and much unemployment. Fortunately, the firm was purchased by enterprising managers who were able to re-open it and employ many of the previous workers. Today it has expanded into a successful commercial centre.

In a sense, it was the carpet factory, replacing the town's largely home-based weaving industry, that heralded a new industrial revival. Naish Felts Ltd, situated in Crow Lane, commenced at Quidhampton in 1800 with the manufacture of corduroy. Until that time John Brasher rented the old Wilton textile mill but, following the destruction of his plant during the wave of agricultural discontent known as the Swing Riots, he was probably relieved to hand over the lease to John Naish in 1835.

By 1850 Naish had branched into piano felt, the product that was to reach worldwide markets. Today, the recently refurbished mill, with members of the Naish family still involved, imports felt from Germany and has diversified into a whole range of modern products from industrial gaskets to indoor bowling greens. In 1975 a much greater diversification was started into hand-washing machines.

Wilton felt mill in the early 1900s. This is the hand felting shop where men worked in pairs to produce piano hammer felt. A large steam engine was installed to keep the machines turning, including the drive shaft, wheels and belts which can be seen.

George Brewer made his transition from journeyman blacksmith to agricultural implement maker in the second half of the 19th century. In 1861 he was in charge of the machinery at the felt mill where he was once forced to stop activities so that a young boy, Samuel Leabourne, could be got out of the belts. The boy later died from his injuries. By 1881 the census described George as a 'smith machinist', employing six men and a boy. Like his contemporary Peter Parmiter at Tisbury, he had an inventive mind. Farmers were demanding more from a blacksmith than the shoeing of horses and the repair of wagons. By 1906, when his son Albert became mayor, the firm had developed dramatically, producing a wide range of agricultural implements. Although the firm was sold in 1912, subsequent owners retained the family name and the business continued to prosper until the 1980s.

Perhaps the most colourful and well-documented family to reflect Wilton's more recent history is that of Nancy Morland. Her family, the Moores, are first noted in a survey of 1631 and were to create the modern day scrap-recycling firm. Isaac, her great great grandfather, was born in Wilton in 1792 where, as a member of the Wiltshire Volunteers, he helped guard French prisoners on their way to Dartmoor. Coming from a family of weavers, he continued this trade and moved to the wealthier town of Westbury to improve his prospects. Here he met and married Margaret Dodimead. However, the 1829 Weavers' Strike forced him to return with his wife and young family to his grandfather's cottage at Ditchampton.

Here things were no better. The family arrived just as the Swing Riots reached south Wiltshire. In November 1830 Isaac may well have witnessed the disturbances at the Crow Lane mill as rioters destroyed the machines used for wool production. As a result, nine Wilton men joined others from the Pythouse riot in transportation to Australia. So desperate were conditions that, in later years, Isaac's youngest child, John, took employment as a bird scarer.

Wilton at this time was described as 'a very monotonous place, no water works, no lighting except a few greasy old lamps and the pavements of pebble stones'. As the century progressed, Isaac took over the Ditchampton cottage, became a pillar of the Wesleyan Methodist Chapel in North Street and maintained a modest existence. He was a great walker and in old age refused an offer to travel by

opposite] Isaac Moore, who was born in Wilton in 1792 and helped guard French prisoners travelling from Wilton Town Hall to Dartmoor. A cloth weaver by trade, his sons went on to found the scrap merchants business in West Street. A strict Wesleyan Methodist, he was still preaching at Wilton until his death at 92.

train to Devizes, saying that legs were made before railways. In 1884 this remarkable man, then aged ninety-two and living with his daughter at South Newton, was caught in a blizzard after evening preaching in Wilton. He was compelled to shelter under a railway arch and subsequently died of pneumonia. By this time his children were well established in the town.

In 1841 the Pembrokes were involved in two new projects which were to have great influence on the fortunes of the Moore family: the building of a new school in West Street and, opposite, the remarkable Romanesque church built by Lord Herbert of Lea for his mother, the Countess of Pembroke. The demolition of the older buildings on the site presented many opportunities for dealing in wood and other second-hand materials. It was Isaac's elder son, William Vincent Moore, who seized this opportunity and became the first in the family to work

The residence of William Vincent Moore junior and his wife Agnes during the coronation of George V. The house, now three separate shops, is on the corner of Crow Lane and West Street. Agnes (née Carse) came to Wilton as a young woman to live with her uncle, who was clerk of works on the Wilton estate. William was the owner of the scrap merchant business in West Street. They had ten children.

with scrap. He was described as a Marine Store Dealer, trading in old ropes, bottles, rags and bones. An unromantic trade, admittedly, but by 1859, when the Salisbury to Yeovil Railway became the second railway to stop at Wilton, he was granted a free pass over the entire region because of the considerable trade he was bringing them.

Moore Brothers workshops at Ditchampton around 1924. It was originally a filling station and car stockist, but during the 2nd World War, when petrol was rationed, they were not selected as a supplier. In consequence the business was diverted to reconditioning engines.

The firm's success has always depended on its ability to diversify according to the market's requirements. By 1970 the need for a more fundamental change was recognised. Instead of merely buying and selling on, machines were installed for the processing and recycling of waste materials to meet the needs of the modern economy. Throughout this long period the family retained control and continued to play a full part in the affairs of the town, but at the turn of the century the firm was forced into closure.

No study of Wilton life would be complete without reference to Edward Slow, the Wiltshire dialect poet. His father died in 1849 during the cholera epidemic when Edward was seven and his mother, a washerwoman, was forced to move house several times. Nevertheless, she managed to get her son into the highly esteemed Free School in North Street (now Moat House). Here he was clothed, educated and given a bag of tools to start his apprenticeship with Silas Burt, a wheelwright and coach builder in Salisbury. He later returned to Wilton to work with Mark Stone, adjacent to Brewers, before commencing a coach-building business of his own.

Described as 'a man of rugged face and figure and with a loud resonant voice', Slow's business was sufficiently successful for him to retire by the late 1890s. He served with the first William Moore on the newly constituted

The Moat House, Wilton. Previously the home of the Free School, it is now a private residence.

borough council and, like him, was twice mayor. By then his dialect verses were well known, having appeared in a series of six volumes from 1867 to 1898. His poetic version of 'The Wiltshire Moonrakers', based on a much older legend, became a national symbol of the old Wiltshireman's ability to disguise rustic astuteness beneath a simple, rugged exterior. His descriptions of sights, sounds and characters have left us with a clearer picture of the Wilton of his day and in a dialect which, sadly, is no longer heard.

'Ower Girt Zeptember Vair', for example, reminds us that the chief west of England sheep fairs of the 19th century were held at Wilton, events that continue, though in less rumbustious form, today:

> Of ael naizes an zenes in tha country that are,
> Ther's nuthen ta beat ower girt Zeptember vair;
> Var hussle, an bussle, an tussle, we man an wie be-ast,
> It can vie wie any in tha country at least.
> Now if ya da dout it, com an zee var yer-zelf,
> An be here day avore, Zeptember tha twelth.

Slow's rhymes were hardly great poetry but were much admired by Edith Olivier whose own background as the daughter of the Wilton rector, Canon Dacres Olivier, was as different as the proverbial Wiltshire chalk and cheese. Canon Dacres' household was dominated by stern Victorian values, with cast-iron rules for every aspect of domestic life. In the large Georgian rectory (just east of the modern one) even the roses were picked and displayed under his personal supervision:

> Every evening, sheets of newspaper were laid upon the long polished tables in the hall, and soup plates filled with water were placed upon these. Here the roses rested when they first came in. It took hours to arrange them; and, in the house as in the garden, my father would not allow his pets to be used merely for decoration. Each flower must be given its solitary honour, and the vases he preferred were simple specimen glasses in which a single bloom could sit in undisturbed beauty, its perfect form controlled by a vase which exactly fitted it.

Edith had yearned for a career in the theatre but, knowing how much her brother Arthur's venture in this direction had distressed her father, she resigned herself to local amateur dramatics and a life of civic endeavour. At the Daye House, however, situated in Wilton Park, she later drew about her a coterie of brilliant young artists. Like the Bloomsbury Set, they left their mark on the English cultural scene: Siegfried Sassoon, Cecil Beaton and Lord David Cecil all achieved critical acclaim. William Walton commenced his first symphony at the Daye House. Rex Whistler, the artist who was tragically killed in the Second World War, was a special friend who wrote amusing letters and illustrated her books. Edith's own writing never brought her the literary fame and financial security she desired but *Without Knowing Mr Walkley*, written in 1939, gives a fascinating view of her early life in and around Wilton.

In 1934 Edith was elected to Wilton Town Council, its first woman councillor, and became its first woman mayor four years later at the outbreak of war. Her diaries reveal how hard she worked to achieve respect in this role. She died in 1948 at the age of seventy and was buried in Wilton parish churchyard.

It was Edith Olivier who encouraged A G Street to develop from an obscure country farmer to an author and broadcaster of note. Arthur Street was born in 1892 with his feet apparently facing the wrong way. Painful operations to right this during his youth may well explain the sturdy determination he adopted to succeed as a farmer during the

Ditchampton Farm, home of the farmer, broadcaster and writer A.G. Street

post-First World War depression when many others failed. Taking over his father's tenant farm at Ditchampton, he radically altered the traditional farming pattern to avoid bankruptcy He stopped growing corn and put the land down to grass. With his wife Vera, the daughter of the felt mill manager, he started up a milk round in Wilton and Salisbury doing the deliveries himself. This meant rising at 4.30 am, seven days a week, and, with only one labourer, milking a herd of seventy cows by the revolutionary method of open-air dairy farming described earlier.

A.G. Street (centre) organised a 'ghost' darts match for the BBC about 1938. Several pubs, including this one, the Black Horse at Teffont, took part. From left to right: Jim Yeates, Charlie Stanley, A.G. Street, Bill Gillingham, Stan Lappage.

In 1929, irritated by an incompetent article on farming in the *Daily Mail,* he submitted a piece himself. To his astonishment it was accepted and he continued to write regularly for the *Farmers' Weekly* and *Salisbury Times* until the end of his life. His first book, *Farmer's Glory,* was written in 1932, at the suggestion of Edith Olivier who was impressed by his articles. It was based on his own and his father's experiences at Ditchampton Farm and was an instant success. He went on to write over 30 books, mostly concerned with rural life during the next three decades.

Street was clearly not afraid of work. His daughter, Pamela, in her own biography of her father, tells us he wrote at night after a working day that often began at 4 am. From 1933 he commenced a broadcasting career and soon became a popular member of the *Any Questions?* panel. From this platform he commented with humour and customary bluntness on the state of agriculture and current events in general.

Wilton looks back with pride on a civic history that spans nine centuries. In recent times its industrial base and attraction to tourism have been supplemented by the development of the British Army headquarters, now Land Command, probably its largest employer of civilian labour. Its removal to Andover in 2008 will undoubtedly cause hardships, but it is to be hoped that the increasing number of small commercial units in the outlying industrial centre, as well as the town, will bring new opportunities.

Wilton lost its borough status in 1974 – a cause of much regret in the town – and there is a danger that the projected changes in local government may push it further into the shadow of the city of Salisbury. Nevertheless, Wilton retains an active local council and a friendly community. It will be interesting to see how it deals with the new challenges of the 21st century.

Bibliography

The general section at the beginning contains a few sources which are important to the whole or large parts of the text. It also includes books which have provided interesting or helpful background reading. Sources relevant to each village are then listed separately.

The Victoria County History of Wiltshire, vols III (1956), VI (1962), VIII (1965), XI (1980) and XIII (1987)

Census Returns for Nadder Valley villages, 1871, 1881, 1891 and 1901

Kelly's *Directories* 1855-1939

Department of the Environment Listed Buildings – Salisbury District 1985-6

Pevsner N., *The Buildings of England: Wiltshire* (Penguin, 1963, 2nd edn, 1975)

Mee A., *Wiltshire* (Hodder & Stoughton, 1939, new edn, 1965)

Cheetham J.H. and Piper J.N., *Wiltshire* (a Shell Guide, 1968)

Woodruffe B., *Wiltshire Villages* (Robert Hale, 1982)

Marshman M., *Wiltshire Village Book* (Countryside Books, 1987)

Kidd A., *Down Your Way*, vols 1 and 2 *(Salisbury Journal*, 1988-90)

The Donheads

Donhead WI Scrapbook 1956

Godfrey, Rev. John, *The Parish of Donhead St Andrew* (privately published 1977)

Donhead Newsletters (Australian Association of Donhead Descendants, 1985-7)

Nina, Duchess of Hamilton and Brandon, *The Chronicles of Ferne* (Animal Defence Society, 1951)

Chafin W, *Anecdotes and History of Cranbourn Chase*

(1818, reprint: Dovecote Press, 1991)

Hawkins D., *Cranborne Chase* (Gollancz, 1980)

Semley

Semley WI Scrapbook 1956

Johnson, Canon A., *church pamphlet* (1988)

Bournemouth Evening Echo, 23 March 1968

Hindon

Sheard N., *The History of Hindon* (privately published, 1979)

Hudson WH., *A Shepherd's Life* (Methuen & Co., 1910)

Western Gazette, 28 December 1979

Dewhurst R, *Crosstracks to Hindon* Hobnob Press, 2005

The Fonthills

Fonthill Bishop, Fonthill Gifford and Berwick St Leonard WI Scrapbook 1956

Sheard N., *The History of Hindon* (privately published, 1979)

Jackson R., 'The Lords of Fonthill' (essay, 1974)

Longbourne D., 'William Beckford and Fonthill Abbey'

(Hatcher Review, No. 7, 1979)

Lees-Milne J., *William Beckford* (Compton Russell, 1976)

Mowl T, William Beckford *Western Gazette,* 4 August 1978

Harris R, *Personal Journal*

Tisbury

Miles E., *Tisbury, Past and Present* (privately published, 1920)

Drury J. and P., *A Tisbury History* (Tisbury Books, 1980)

Tisbury Local History Society, *Looking Around Tisbury* (privately published, 1984)

Jackson R., *A History of the Parish Church of St John the Baptist* (privately published, 1973, new edn, 1986)

Jackson R., *The Link Between Tisbury and Chilmark, England and Tisbury and Chilmark, USA* (collected essays, *c.* 1975)

Mould K., *Reflections* (privately published, 1982)

Riggs D.C., *People to Remember – 300 Years in Tisbury and West Tisbury* (Dukes County Historical Society, Mass, USA, 1973)

PJ Parmiter and Son Ltd

1885—1985 (booklet, 1985)

Tisbury Local History Society, *The Tisbury Jubilee Book 2002*

Tisbury Local History Society, *The Tisbook,* 2006

West Tisbury

Drury J. and P., *A Tisbury History* (Tisbury Books, 1980)

Tisbury Local History Society, *Looking Around Tisbury* (privately published, 1984)

Caraman B, *Wardour, A Short History* (privately published, 1984)

Williamson B., *Wardour and the Arundells: Not So Long Ago* (privately published)

Country Houses Assn Ltd, *Pythouse and the Benetts* (published by CHA *c*1987)

Dalton M., 'The Pythouse Riots' *(Hatcher Review* vol 3/30)

Hobsbawn E. and Rude G., *Captain Swing* (Lawrence & Wishart, 1969)

Jackson R., '*Some Glimpses of the West Tisbury Story*' (essay, 1975)

Eyre J, *Pythouse and the Benetts (Country Houses Association,* 2002)

Moody R, *John Benett of Pythouse* (privately published

2003)

Moody R, *Mr Benett of Wiltshire* (Hobnob Press, 2005)

Chilmark

Harfield A.G., *A History of the Village of Chilmark* (privately published, 1961)

Chilmark Quarries, *A Project for European Heritage Year 1975*

Chilmark: A Village Appraisal (Chilmark Parish Council, 1978)

Church pamphlets 1960, 1975 and 1980

Rixon E., Diaries 1904-52 (WSRO, unpublished)

Carnegie I., *England and New England* (privately published, 1993)

The Teffonts

Teffont WI Village History Scrapbook 1956

Parish of Teffont and Churches (church booklet, 1978)

Merrifield C., (private papers, 1992)

Olivier E., *Without Knowing Mr Walkley* (Faber & Faber, 1939)

McBain A, and Nelson L, *The Bounding Spring* (Black Horse Books, 2003)

The Motor, 5 May 1908
Tatler, 27 November 1935

Dinton

Dinton WI and Parish Council Scrapbooks (onwards)

Dinton Church (pamphlet, 1993)

Street P., *A Portrait of Wiltshire* (Robert Hale, 1971)

Western Gazette, 10 November 1978

Baverstock

Saumarez Smith WH., *A History of Baverstock* (privately published, 1984)

Waylen J., *The Highwaymen of Wiltshire* (N.B. Randle, Devizes, 1845)

Gandy I., *Staying with the Aunts* (Harvell Press, 1963)

Barford St Martin

Barford St Martin and Burcombe WI Scrapbook 1953

Church pamphlet (1994)

Manley VS., *Sum of the Ancient Customs Belonging to Wishford and Barford* (publisher unknown, 1630)

Rixon E., Diaries 1904-52 (WSRO, unpublished)

Sawyer R., 'A Real Man of the Tisbury Soil' *(Hatcher Review,* vol 4/35)

Ansty

The Crusader Church, St James, Ansty (church booklet, 1921)

May Day pamphlets (Parish Council, undated)

Western Gazette, 28 July 1961
Salisbury Journal, 9 July 1987

Swallowcliffe

Jenkins S., *Before the Norman Conquest* (privately published, 1972)

The Church of St Peter, Swallowcliffe (privately published, 1976)

Williamson B., *Swallowcliffe – Not So Long Ago* (privately published, undated)

Speake G, *A Saxon Bed Burial on Swallowcliffe Down* (English Heritage, 1989)

Western Gazette, 7 March 1980

Sutton Mandeville

Foston D, (private papers, 1993)

Church pamphlet (1993)

Fovant

Clay R C C, *History of Fovant* (privately published 1967)

Nuttall R, *History of Fovant* (privately published 1981)

Combes L., (compiled) *Badges in the Chalk* (privately published, undated)

Wilts Archaeological Magazine, vol 66 (1971)

Salisbury Journal, 4 March 1971

Salisbury Journal, 31 December 1992

Pages from our History by the people of Fovant (Hobnob Press, 2005)

Compton Chamberlayne

Memorials of Old Wiltshire (Bemrose and Son 1906)

Woolrych A H, *Penruddocke's Rising in the West* (The Historical Society 1955)

Church pamphlet (1993)

Wilts Archaeological Magazine, vols 13 (1872), 14 (1874) and 15 (1875)

Parish Council Minute Book (1897)

Burcombe

Barford St Martin and Burcombe WI Scrapbook 1953

Rundle P., (private papers, 1993)

Street A.G., *Farmer's Glory* (Faber & Faber, 1932)

Wilton

Haslam J., *Anglo-Saxon Towns in Southern England* (Phillimore, 1984)

Boulter E.J., *A Short History of Wilton* (privately published, 1981)

Rousell C., *Wilton* (Alan Sutton, 1993)

Morland N., *The Reclaimers* (unpublished, 1985)

Morland T.E., *A New Chronology of Wilton* (privately published, 1987)

Slow E., *Wiltshire Rhymes for the West Countrie* (R.R. Edwards, 1903)

Chandler J., *Figgetty Pooden, the Dialect Verse of Edward Slow* (Wilts Library & Museum Service, 1982)

Olivier E., *Without Knowing Mr Walkley* (Faber & Faber, 1939)

Middelboe P., *Edith Olivier from Her Journals 1924-48* (Weidenfeld & Nicolson, 1989)

Street P., *My Father* (Robert Hale, 1969, 2nd edn, 1984)

Salisbury Journal, 12 May 1983

Salisbury Times, 13 February 1984

Salisbury Times, 24 February 1986

Acknowledgements

The generous assistance I have been given whilst involved in this project has been overwhelming. If I have inadvertently failed to record my appreciation to anyone I hope they will forgive me.

Mrs Marion Andrews – Toby Baker – Barford Inn, Barford St Martin – Mrs PV Barnes – Benett Arms, Semley – Basil Bevis – Mrs T. Blakeman – John Blanchard –John Boulter – Miss Joyce Bowker – Mrs Pamela Bown – Mrs Heather Cassidy – Robert Chalke – Mrs Violet Cheverell – Ewart Clark – Mrs Dorothy Clay – Alan Clayton – Jack Combes – Mick and Sue Combes – Mrs Margaret Cowgill – Lance Croasdaile – Dr Mary Dalton – Peter Daniels – Derek Dawkins – Mrs Margaret Dunn – Miss Elizabeth Ellis –

Linda and Duncan Ellis – Patrick Faithfull – Jack Feltham – Mrs Aileen Fisher-Roe – John Flower – Miss Diana Forbes – David Foston – Mrs Louisa George – Mrs Gladys Gipson – Mrs Mary Godfrey – Miss May Gray – Ron Gray – Jim Green —Martin Green – Miss Muriel Harding – Bob Hardy – Charles Hardy – Mary and Charles Hare – Maj. T. Mordaunt Hare – Percy Hare – Reg Harris – Anthony Harriss – Mrs Hilda Hayter – Mrs Vi Head – Mrs Doris Hill – Hindon Archives – Brenda and Mike Hobbs – Mrs Kathleen Jackson – John Jeffery – Mrs Helen Jenkins – Mrs Joyce Jenkyns – Canon Anthony Johnson – Mrs Joyce Johnson – Tony Keating – Gordon Lake – Willie Langdon – Ernie Langford – Mrs James Leasor – Miss Alice Lee – Bill Lockyer – Mrs Mary Lovell – Mrs Mollie Mabey – Mrs Barbara McCoy – Miss Sal Margetts – Charlie Merrifield – Nancy and Tim Morland – Hon. Mrs Clare Morrison – Mrs Kathleen Mould – David Muir – Miss Margaret Mullins – Miss Olive Mullins – John Naish – Lady Nepean – Mrs Sylvia Newbury – J F Newman —Roy Nuttall – Mrs Joan Parsons – Les Parsons – Fred Peckham – Mrs Agnes Penny – Mrs K.M. Plumb – Tony and Gill Rose – Chris Rousell – Mrs Mary Ruffell – Percy Rundle – Miss Daisy Shallcross – Miss Phyllis Sharples – Miss Norah Sheard – Peter Simmonds – Roy Simper – W.H. Saumarez Smith – Freddie Spenser – Monica Stone – Tisbury Archives

I should also like to pay tribute to the Women's Institute Scrapbooks within this valley and nationally. Without them a great deal of local history would probably have been lost.

Index

This index includes most places and persons (excluding monarchs) referred to in the text and captions. Captions are indexed according to the pages on which they appear, not necessarily the page of the illustration to which they refer. Principal parish references are given in **bold** type.

Index

Index